Charles Price, Jr. on first tee
at Sunnehanna Country Club
in early 1920s.

The History of Sunnehanna Country Club
and
The Sunnehanna Amateur

Researched and Written
by
John Yerger III

Contributions by George Wolfe

Dedication

Dedicated to Amateur Golf

BIBLIOGRAPHY

BOOKS

A Centennial Tribute to Golf in Philadelphia by James Finnegan; *A Century of Golf in Western Pennsylvania, Americas Industrial Heritage Project - Pennsylvania;Golf in America* by George Pepper and the Editors of Golf Magazine; *Grandview Cemetary, A Historical Overview 1885-1995; Seventeenth Annual Convention League of Cities; The Third Class 1916; The Architects of Golf* by Geoffrey Cornish and Ron Whitten; *The Course Beautiful, Reminiscences of the Links, Gleanings from the Wayside* by A.W. Tillinghast, research and design by Richard C. Wolfe, Robert Trebus and Stuart F. Wolfe; *The Masters* by Furman Bisher; *The Golden Age of Golf Design* by Geoff Shackelford; *The Walker Cup 1922 to 1929 : Golf's Finest Contest* by Gordon Simmonds; *Golf Architecture in America: It's Strategy and Construction* by George Thomas; *The Links* by Robert Hunter; *Baltusrol: 100 years* by Richard C. Wolfe, RobertTrebus and Stuart Wolffe.

NEWSPAPERS

Johnstown Tribune Democrat, Latrobe Bulletin, Pittsburgh Press, Reading Eagle, Pittsburgh Tribune Review.

MAGAZINES

Golf World, Golf Week, Golf Digest, The Iron Trade Review.

OTHER SOURCES

The Cambria County Library: David Glosser Library Johnstown Area Heritage Association, The Hagley Museum, Borough of Westmont, United State Golf Association.

INDIVIDUALS

John Goettlicher, Mr. & Mrs. Charles Price, Mr. & Mrs. Louis Heinze, Mr. & Mrs. Chuck Mamula, Mr. Ed Haberkorn, Mr. & Mrs. Clayton Dovey, Mr. John Mills, Mr. Frank Kiraly, Mr. Charles Kunkle, Mr. Bob Hahn, Mr. Bobby Greenwood, Mr. Joe Campbell, Dr. Ed Updegraff, Mr. Don Cherry, Dr. Robert Reilly, Mr. & Mrs. William Crooks.

PHOTOGRAPHS

Chuck Mamula, Dan McKean

Library of Congress Catalog Number: 2004107814

Designed by Treewolf Productions, Basking Ridge, New Jersey

ISBN 0-9651818-6-3

Printed by Smith Lithographic Corporation, Rockville, Maryland

Contents

Foreword

The history of Sunnehanna Country Club is rich and deep, yet a formal written compendium of its eighty-year existence had never been bound prior to this publication. The daunting task of researching, compiling and drafting an eight-decade history presented many obstacles, most notably the absence of a central source for historical references and photographs. In formulating Sunnehanna's history book, the author did not have the benefit of interviews and pictures of the designers of the golf course and Clubhouse, A. W. Tillinghast and Henry Rogers. Similarly, first hand accounts of the activities of our Founding Members were obscured by time.

George Wolfe,
Club President 2003
and Tom Stephenson,
Club President 2004.

Fortunately, our golf course and Clubhouse architects have interesting biographies and have left legacies of their work that eases the researchers burden. Likewise, the Founding Members of Sunnehanna were at the helm of businesses at the forefront of world industry. These people and institutions form a compelling story in and of themselves and tell the story of Johnstown at the height of the industrial age. Also, the first hand reporting of Sunnehanna Member Charles Kunkle, Jr., provided a continuum from 1936 to the present. We would like to thank Mr. Kunkle for his generosity, research, support and encouragement. A sincere thanks is also owed to all our Members who contributed to this book and provided their support to the project.

In many ways, this book is volume one of a history that could grow to encyclopedic levels. Every facet of the Club's history sparks separate stories that could not be fully pursued or told in the confines of these pages. For instance, the quintessential look at Tillinghast's life and writings is a three-volume trilogy published by Treewolf Productions. Certainly, the reader will get a flavor of this diverse history and will recognize the digressions many of the people, places and time provoke.

Our deepest thanks to John Yerger for his unflinching dedication to this project. John devoted countless hours in canvassing the microfilm records of the *Tribune-Democrat*, the archives in Pennsylvania Room at the Cambria County Library, the USGA Library in Far Hills, New Jersey and many related sources. Simply put, this book would not have been written without John Yerger's creativity and determination.

Although Sunnehanna has hosted fifty-one Sunnehanna Amateurs and two decades of the Invitational preceding it, the Club has been primarily a refuge for its Members. In true country club fashion, golf, swimming, tennis, bowling, bridge, gin, hearts and gourmet dining have all been an integral part of the Sunnehanna experience. The current Board Of Governors and supporting Membership have all sought to preserve Sunnehanna's history and we can be very proud of the golf course and Clubhouse in our eighty-first year.

On Behalf of The Board Of Governors
and Members, Past and Present

Acknowledgments

John Yerger, III

The idea of a book about Sunnehanna Country Club came out of a larger goal: creating a historical document that told a unique and important story in American golf. The Sunnehanna Amateur was the nation's first major medal play tournament and changed national amateur competition. Sunnehanna's golf course was influenced by two of American golf's greatest architects, initially designed by Albert Warren Tillinghast, and then later William Flynn modestly altered the original design. Another goal was to incorporate the steel industry's historical influence on golf in Johnstown. Sunnehanna Country Club, like many clubs across the nation, remains one of the few vestiges of the halcyon days of industrial America.

This project took shape conceptually six years ago. Then a member of the Sunnehanna Amateur committee, I undertook several initiatives to document the tournament's important place in golf. The first step was recovering and cataloguing the tournament's photographic history which was largely ignored and underutilized. Vivid evidence of golf's greatest players in their formative years now adorns the clubhouse walls. The tournament program was another element. It provided historical information that previously had been unavailable. In doing research for the program, I became interested in the history of the Sunnehanna Invitational and in the process uncovered exhibitions by Sarazen, Didrickson, and Hagan, among others. This led to a more ambitious goal: a document that was forever an important history in American golf. The Sunnehanna Amateur program of 2001 was done to make the case for this initiative; it succeeded. After the tournament, Charles Kunkle, Jr. queried various members about the idea of supporting a book. Based on the positive response, more than eighty members provided the initial seed money for the project.

A format was adopted that could optimally use the photographic history that existed. A major problem was what didn't exist: almost no tournament photos before 1974 and in some years no photos at all. The Club's photographic history was difficult and was exacerbated by the Flood of 1977 which destroyed the newspapers photographic negatives. Thankfully, three people provided assistance: John Goettlicher, Judy Heinze and Bob Reilly. Goettlicher, Sunnehanna's head professional from 1965-1982, collected years worth on newspaper clippings and photographs. Heinze had saved photos and files her father, Julius Eckel, had accumulated as editor of the Club's monthly newsletter. Reilly provided a first tee photo of the greatest historical significance, a 16-year old Jack Nicklaus.

On a personal note, I would like to thank the following: John Goettlicher for his belief in this book and a similar love of the game, my parents for their patience and support, Lesley Suppes for tolerating my writing ineptitude and Chuck Mamula whose timeless photos from 1974 on can now be seen. A special thanks goes to Bob Trebus, whose Herculean effort, encouragement and daily communications made this a special book; on behalf of Sunnehanna Country Club, and myself, "Thank You, Bob".

I hope you are enlightened by this extraordinary history of American amateur golf and the Sunnehanna Country Club.

Golf in Johnstown
and
Sunnehanna Country Club

The Johnstown Country Club

The development by Cambria Steel of Yoder Hill began in the aftermath of the Flood. Cambria Steel owned vast farm lands on the hill above Johnstown to grow feed for the mules that worked in their coal mines. The community was originally named Tip Top, as the expansive farm lands were laid out for development by the company. Although financing was available through the corporation, the initial response to living above the city was tepid at best. The steep and winding road was difficult for horse and wagons to climb under the best of conditions. Winter weather or heavy rains made the road impossible to traverse. The decision to build the Inclined Plane in 1890 spurred interest in what was later renamed Westmont. A year later, 1300 travelers on an average day utilized the hillside railway. It also carried horses and wagons on its counter balanced cars up and down the hill every five minutes, every day. The views from above Johnstown were a contrast of the beauty of the surrounding hills against the smoke and haze of industry. At night, the mill's furnaces filled the valley with an incandescent glow. During the day, the benefits of living above the smoke laden air were readily apparent. Westmont's location provided a modest respite from the

industrial haze, as the prevailing westerly wind could push the smog and stench away from the homes perched above.

The large tracts of open land provided recreational opportunities previously unavailable in the cramped quarters of the city. Tennis courts were an early addition to the new community. Another sport that had grabbed the attention of America's burgeoning upper class was golf. In 1888, a year before the tragic events devastated Johnstown, six men met on a hillside cow pasture in Yonkers, New York with six strange implements in hand. Three primitive holes were cut in the field and the game of golf was introduced to a nation. By 1895, the game, initially considered an amusing curiosity was a national obsession. Residents of Westmont were exposed to the game because of their travel for business and pleasure to New York and Philadelphia. In 1895, five youngsters laid out their own links course. George Thackary wrote in 1932, "The three Hamilton's, Dan Stackhouse, and myself started a golf links on the pasture around the old ball grounds and athletics field in Westmont where Luzerne and Tioga Streets now are, with number one tee in front of where Wolle later built his house on Tioga Street. The links extended around the athletic field and beyond the company barn, (later burned)." Before 1895

Introductary page: Golfers play on the third tee at Johnstown Country Club with the memorial to the unkonwn victims of the flood of 1889 in the background (left side).

DESIRABLE BUILDING LOTS
ARE STILL
FOR SALE,
AT PRICES AND TERMS TO SUIT PUR-
CHASERS, IN
Beautiful Westmont.

Valuable Street Improvements have been made by the Company. Many elegant residences have been erected. Advantages of good schools, good neighbors, good order, and good health. Easy and cheap access by Incline Plane. Monthly Tickets, 50 trips, $1. Apply to FRANK M. BUCHANAN, Agent, office at Incline Plane.
CAMBRIA IRON COMPANY.

The Johnstown Country Club

there were less than eighty golf courses in the United States, by the end of the century there were in excess of a thousand.

On April 8, 1903, golf enthusiasts in Johnstown formally organized the Johnstown Country Club. The group secured property known as Old Company Farm from Cambria Steel and adjoined the Johnstown Driving Park. The Driving Park, which opened in 1893, held horse races and equestrian events. Financed with $25,000, the track was a mile and a half long track had stables for fifty horses. Cambria Steel covered almost all costs associated with starting the Club and appointed the vast majority of the Club's Board of Governors. Membership was limited to 100 with a new course laid out over the grounds.

Cambria Steel supported community entities and activities beyond the communities' elite. The company-supported library began in 1870. Later destroyed in the 1889 flood, it was rebuilt with charitable support of Andrew Carnegie. Cambria Steel also started the nation's first run company hospital in 1887 after the state refused to support attempts to start a community facility. The YMCA, the Johnstown Opera House, the Art Institute for

Cambria Free Library

The first Clubhouse of Johnstown Country Club

Women, and the Cambria Library were also beneficiaries of the company's largess. A company town, Cambria Steel's visible support of public institutions was not necessarily altruistic. These acts generated positive publicity and goodwill for the company. It also came with an inferred cost: a benevolent community and work force devoted to the company.

The *Daily Tribune* reported the Club's goal for the upcoming year was to, "...see the grounds and house so fitted as to rival in completeness of their appointments many of the older organizations located near larger cities." The farmhouse was renovated with hardwood floors and the walls papered and decorated. A large fireplace was added in the sitting area and a complete kitchen built. Stables were provided to care for Member's horses. The Club also brought in an "expert ground keeper from Pittsburgh Country Club" to help with the new course. By late May, the course was declared open for play. The nine-hole course was a modest 2646 yards long. To maintain the grounds, the Penn Traffic Company furnished a

Penn Traffic furnished sheep, such as seen here at Essex Country Club, to keep the grass clipped.

flock of sixty sheep to keep the grass kept. When the Club opened, it claimed to have thirty five members: eighteen played in the Club's first tournament on July 4th. The winning low gross score was 67.

By 1906, the growth of Westmont forced changes in the golf course as additional land was needed for housing. Two holes were moved across the Millcreek Road to make way for the community's growth. While the course migrated across the road, another activity was added at the Club: tennis. Room for the courts was made possible by the removal of the race track fence and was placed in the middle of what had been the baseball diamond. The Driving Park had

suffered the same fate as the first golf course: the land was parceled off and sold for development.

The engine for the economy was Cambria Steel which had over 16,000 employees in the Johnstown area. From 1898 to 1912, Cambria Steel invested $70 million dollars in new plants in Johnstown. Its holdings extended beyond the mills and included coal mines that could be found under hillsides throughout the area. Other major employers in the community included Lorain Steel which employed 1300 men. Lorain was a subsidiary of Andrew Carnegie's United States Steel Corporation, which the industrialist formed by consolidating 11 large steel operators in 1901. A subsidiary of Lorain was Johnson Railcar Company, a major manufacturer of steel tracks and switches used for street rail transportation. Suppliers for the steel manufacturers

The Johnstown Country Club

sprung up throughout the region. Haws Refractory employed 400 men and made bricks that lined the walls of the furnaces used in the steel making process. Their silica bricks displaced imported bricks from Wales and England and were in demand throughout the United States. The other major employer in the region, other than steel, was coal. While coal, and its by-product coke, was an integral product in the production of steel, it was the principle fuel used to produce electricity and to heat homes across America. These were heady times for the community and business leaders.

With the continuing economic growth in Johnstown and growing demand for housing, Johnstown Country Club was forced to move. An entirely new course was built across the Millcreek Road in 1908. The course was designed by George Thackary and was considerably longer than its predecessor measuring 3,104 yards. The course, like most courses in golf's early years, was primitive at best. Maintenance was modest. Large mounds, known as chocolate drops, dotted Johnstown Country Club's course as did earthen mounds. Two six-foot high "chocolate drops" were on the course's third hole. Chocolate drops were a practical solution to cover stones accumulated during construction and maintenance. The stones were stacked, then covered with dirt, hence the name. These hazards were a familiar sight on courses throughout the country.

Tennis also took hold at the Club. The Club sponsored its first major tournament and received fifty-two entrants. In the doubles finals, John Gocher and E.L. Vinson defeated George Suppes and Conrad Suppes. Both Suppes' became prominent players and promoters

Chocolate drops like these at Somerset Hills could be found on the Johnstown Country Club links.

The Johnstown Country Club

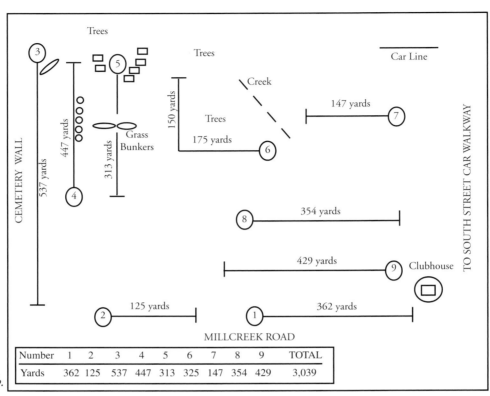

Number	1	2	3	4	5	6	7	8	9	TOTAL
Yards	362	125	537	447	313	325	147	354	429	3,039

The original layout for Johnstown Country Club.

of tennis in Johnstown for many years. Matches took place regularly with the Johnstown Tennis Club which played on the six courts at The Mound in Westmont.

With the golf course already moved, the Club's Board decided a new clubhouse was needed. In March of 1910, the Club hired Henry Rogers, who was responsible for many of the prominent new homes in Westmont. His work could also be found on several community buildings including The Grove, which regularly held dances. The mission style clubhouse was larger

View of Johnstown Country Club
Golf Links and Clubhouse

The Johnstown Country Club

than its predecessor. Paid for by Cambria Steel, which also covered the cost of building the new course, the clubhouse was erected against a gently sloping hillside. A seventy-five foot porch looked out over the course. The Club hired a professional, J.J O'Brien from Pittsburgh to assist with golfing activities and course maintenance.

Jock Hutchison won the PGA Championship in 1920 and theBritish Open in 1921. He played in the first official tournament at Johnstown Country Club in 1910.

In September, the Club sponsored an open tournament hoping to attract professional golfers playing in the tenth Western Open at Beverly Country Club in Chicago. The tournament details were handled by Hoover Bankard. An executive with Cambria Steel, Bankard was a fine player who had played in several national tournaments. It was hoped that the purse of $200 was sufficient to attract the likes of Willie Anderson, first major player to dominate golf in America winning four U.S. Opens between 1901 and 1905, Laurence Autcherlonie; and Pittsburgh golfers, Dave Robertson and Jock Hutchinson among others. The tournament was considered one of the biggest sporting events ever in the area. Jock Hutchinson, the two-time West Penn Open champion, claimed the first place prize of $75. The head professional at Pittsburgh Golf Club, Hutchinson's thirty-six hole score of 152 was four strokes ahead of J. J. O'Brien with Oakmont's Robertson and Jack Dingwall finishing third. O'Brien received a runner-up check worth $30 for two days of work. Another prominent professional in the field was Fred Brand from Allegheny Country Club. Brand, the 1904 Scottish Open champion, had also won the 1905 and 1908 West Penn Open titles.

The Club continued to grow, used by top officials of Cambria Steel, selected community members, and the scions of the American Steel industry. Andrew Carnegie and Henry Clay Frick visited as did Loretto native Charles Schwab. Schwab picked up the game of golf in 1915. When construction of his vast summer estate–Immergrun–began Schwab hired Donald Ross to build a private nine-hole course. When completed, Schwab's summer home was considered the finest estate in the United States. The golf course, called Eurana, challenged visitors of all abilities, including Bobby Jones.

A meeting of steel officials in 1917.

Johnstown Country Club's list of activities grew with time. Golf was certainly the prime activity. Dr. James Jefferson won his second straight club

The Johnstown Country Club

Player tees-off while homes go up in Westmont.

championship in record fashion. In the semi-finals, Jefferson was three-over after four holes and three down. He played the next five holes in three-under par. Jefferson's even-par nine score of 35 tied the course record. The Club also added increasingly popular tournament to its schedule: a Scotch-Foursome. Tournaments were perpetually taking place over the Club's links. Inter-club matches with the Greensburg Country Club, the Blairmont Country Club in Altoona, and the Uniontown Country Club were ongoing and frequent with members traveling by rail. Trap or skeet shooting was added, as well as an outdoor band shell to serenade members on summer evenings. Indoors, the male members utilized the hallways for an unintended purpose: bowling. But the Club was not always used as a place of leisure.

Johnstown Country Club was a place of idle pleasures for the communities' elite and the company's upper management. But the passage of the Volsted Act in 1919 ended one pleasure: a drink. In preparation for the "July Thirst", users stocked up. In two days, one dealer in Johnstown sold 50 barrels of whiskey and $10,000 of libation in a week. Liquor dealers complained of exhaustion from the pressure of Prohibitionists and brisk demand for their product. The Cambria Distillery in Cambria City prepared for a new day, converting its operation into a soft drink factory and changing its name to Johnstown Bottling Company. Today the former distillery is used for ethnic arts.

For the Johnstown's workers, a beer after work was the least of their concerns. The obvious economic prosperity generated by World War I created new expectations for the pre-war immigrants from Europe. Strong supporters of the war effort, they purchased liberty bonds and enlisted in large numbers for military service. Discriminated against prior to the war, the immigrants hoped their devotion to their adopted country during the war would result in acceptance. They were wrong. The realization that the concept of freedom and democracy ended at work and in their communities led to anger and resentment.

The Great Steel Strike of 1919 was the first challenge by organized labor of the employer-worker relationship that existed in Johnstown. For unified union support during World War I, the government pressured industrial America to recognize unions and collective bargaining. When workers were approached by organizers about union representation, thousands of workers responded enthusiastically. They hoped organizing would give them a voice with the company and offered hope of a better future. A strike ensued after

The Johnstown Country Club

COUNTRY CLUB HOUSE, JOHNSTOWN, PA.

the steel companies refused to even recognize the union's right to represent workers, let alone their demands. Among the union's demands was the elimination of the 12-hour workday. In September of 1919, steelworkers throughout the nation voted to strike. Over 300,000 men left work, the largest work stoppage in the nation's history. The companies responded in a variety of nefarious ways. In Johnstown, Midvale Steel and Ordinance, which bought Cambria Steel in 1915, utilized Johnstown Country Club's clubhouse as a police station. Hired policeman and their horses bivouacked at the Club. Company heads and police leadership planned protection of the company's facilities and activities against the striking workers from within its walls. By year's end, the strike had been broken. Union organizers and their supporters were run out of town.

Two years after the strike, a major announcement was made: Johnstown Country Club would move again. The continued growth of Westmont made the Club's current location precarious. In all likelihood, Midvale Steel planned to use the golf course for housing. After discussions with the steel company, the Club secured a site known as Cambria Farms for its new location. The Club adopted a new charter and new name, Sunnehanna Country Club. Activities continued for two years while construction took place at the new location. On August 29, 1923, the final tournament was played on the Club's course, an inter-club match with Greensburg Country Club. Parts of the abandoned Club's grounds were developed. Westmont Upper-Yoder High School used the former fairways for its football games. The Club's locker rooms were used to change after practice and for games.

Later, the Club operated under the name of Ye' Olde Country Club. The Club's membership was limited to Bethlehem Steel's middle and upper management. It offered dining and tennis to its members. Bethlehem Steel's desperate financial condition forced the company to jettison non-essential assets and close the Club.

The topography around the former clubhouse has changed dramatically since it opened in 1908. But today, one can look out the windows and envision watching a leisurely game over gently rolling hills, refreshment in hand, and smoke emanating from the valley below.

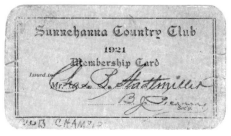

The Genesis of the
Sunnehanna Country Club

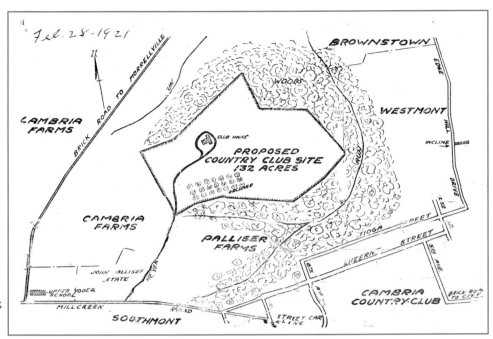

The Johnstown Ledger, February 28, 1921.

While activities continued at Cambria Country Club, work started on the finding a new location. Board members John Ogden, Supervisor of Steel Operations for Cambria Steel, led a group responsible for finding suitable land. The Club anticipated that its grounds would be used for development as boroughs of Westmont and Southmont grew. Members had wistfully looked west toward a hillside farm owned by Cambria Steel.

Known as Cambria Farms, the land was unlike anything else in Johnstown. Views from the crown of the hill provided unending views of the Laurel Highlands. To the north was a relatively unobstructed view of the 1700-foot deep Conemaugh Gap. The proposed new locations 132 acres would enable the Club to construct a badly needed eighteen hole golf course and room for additional amenities.

A New Charter and a New Name

An agreement was made with Cambria Steel to lease the land for $1.00 a year for twenty-five years. Quickly work began on the golf course. A.W. Tillinghast, one of golf's pre-eminent architects was

Aerial of Sunnehanna Country Club in the top left corner. Remnants of Cambria Country Club are also in view.

hired to design it. The Club's goal was to have the course and clubhouse opened on July 4, 1923. While work progressed on the course, the Board adopted a new charter, and a new name. The name Sunnehanna was the Native American name for the river now known as the Stoneycreek, it meant "slow moving stream". The Board also decided to finance the Club, issuing $50,000 worth of debt in denominations of $100. The Club also established a class of members known as "Life Membership" for $1,000 each. Life members were afforded all privileges for infinitum. Initiation fees for new members were $150 until August 1, 1921, $200 thereafter. By September, the Board moved forward with construction of the club-house.

Henry Rogers was hired to design the clubhouse in January of 1922 for $2,500. A prominent architect in Johnstown, Rogers had designed many of the grand homes on Tioga Street and Luzerne Street. The construction estimate was $80,000 and included bowling alleys, a swimming pool and tennis courts, which could be flooded in the winter for ice skating. The Club built a bridal path around the perimeter of the course, using the existing barn for member's horses. The barn, erected before the turn of the century, was part of Cambria Iron's farm that raised grain for the company mules.

By May of 1923, significant progress had been made on the course and the clubhouse. Furniture and lighting fixtures costing $13,457 were ordered from Marshall Fields in Chicago through Penn Traffic.

The Opening

On September 8, 1923, Sunnehanna Country Club opened. Out-of-town members traveled to Johnstown in their private Pullman Cars for the grand opening. Sixty players played in the first golf tournament. A large audience surrounded the swimming pool and watched an aquatics show. Inside, an orchestra furnished music for dancing. Others milled about the Club's corridors spending time in the billiards room and the bowling alleys.

While the golf course came in under budget, the same could not be said for the clubhouse. The final cost was significantly higher than the budget.

Total Clubhouse Expense	$95,210.88
Swimming Pool	$6,416.70
Water, Power and Phone Lines	$4457.31
Septic Tank and Sewer	$1851.35
Bowling Alleys	$2816.20
Total	**$110,752.44**

To help with the Club's massive start up costs and alleviate the debt, Bethlehem Steel provided, $25,000 which in return it received transferable memberships and the caveat that the Club raised matching funds.

Sunnehanna Country Club

Bethlehem Steel was the creation of Loretto native Charles Schwab, who joined Sunnehanna in 1927. One of the country's wealthiest individuals, his estimated net worth was in excess of $300 million dollars. Schwab's strong ties to the community led to significant investment in the local steel making facility. From 1924 to 1926, Bethlehem Steel invested about $35 million in new plant and equipment. As Schwab stated from his summer estate in Loretto in 1926, " Johnstown is perhaps not the best place in the world for a steelworks (but) so long as I have money or can borrow money I am going to make Cambria Steel works one of the greatest in the world because it is here in Cambria County."

BRILLIANCE ATTENDS OPENING OF NEW HOME OF SUNNEHANNA COUNTRY CLUB

Activities Abound

When it was completed, Sunnehanna Country Club was a source of pride for the members and community. The spectacular views coupled with the course, swimming pool, tennis courts, bridal path, and clubhouse, rivaled other big city clubs.

Activities abounded at the Club. Luncheon and bridge parties sponsored by woman members made the social pages. *The Tribune* reported on one such event, "44 guest at a luncheon at the Sunnehanna Country Club, honored Miss Taylor. Italian forget-me-nots, zinnias, gladiolas, and flox were in low flower bowls decorating the long table in a C- shape. Eleven tables of bridge were arranged following the luncheon with awards of exquisite pieces of chiffon and lace personals."

Tennis privileges were available to members for $3.00 per year or for 50 cents a day. Matches with the Johnstown Tennis Club continued.

Regularly, an orchestra filled the Club's walls with the finest in classical music. Programs included the work of Mozart, Schubert, Puccini, Stebbins, and Mendelssohn. Guest musicians from two of the nation's finest music school, the Peabody School of Music in Baltimore and The Curtis Institute in Philadelphia, made appearances.

Putting on the second green, 1924.

For the men, Stag Smokers was a night without the other half. The evening included four, six-round boxing matches, billiards, bowling, cards and refreshments. These testosterone-filled evenings proved to wildly popular.

Financial Realities

In spite of all these activities, a year after it opened, Sunnehanna Country Club struggled under the weight of its massive debt. In response, the Club sent a letter to members explaining the necessity of an assessment of $50 per member. It was summarily voted down by the members. The cost of the Woman's Saturday luncheon was increased from $.50 to $1.00. The Club's dining room had lost $1,000 per month since it opened. By year's end, the Club was $65,980 in debt.

In 1925, the Board approved a budget that included no funds for course maintenance: "You will notice no provision for maintenance of the golf course, in so far as materials or greens keepers are concerned. These are one of the things that will vary from month-to-month and should not be contracted for until the available funds are in sight." Dues were increased for the Club's 400 active members by $20 per year, junior and woman members by $10. The Board hoped to raise $12,800 and substantially reduce the Club's yawning debt.

The schedule of events remained the same: golf leading the way. Interclub matches for men and woman regularly took place. Parties of all types were held at the Club, the most successful of the season a "Baby Party" at which prizes were awarded to members with the best costume. A special note was made that "at intermission a Charleston exhibition was staged," referring to the dance craze that defined the period.

1927: A Busy Year

Nineteen twenty-seven was a busy year at Sunnehanna and in the community. Strong fiscal years in 1925 and 1926 improved the Club's balance sheet. The reduced debt permitted the hiring of a full-time golf

Sunnehanna Country Club

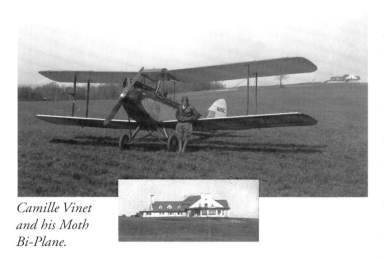

Camille Vinet and his Moth Bi-Plane.

course superintendent, Walter Anderson. Anderson, who trained under nationally known Emil Loeffler at Oakmont Country Club, was busy preparing the course for the coming year in 1927. Anderson had his hands full. The Club's budget restrictions and mistakes in construction led to numerous problems, specifically fairways and greens starved of grass. To deal with the dilemma, the Club enlisted the talents of Anderson's mentor to provide expert advice.

While Anderson and Loeffler toiled on the course, above it the members were entertained almost daily by stunt pilots at the adjoining Stutzman Airfield. America's fever for flight was ignited after men returned home from World War I. The airfield was used for airmail delivery and by flying enthusiasts. Candy from H.K. Love, who owned Sunshine Candy's in Johnstown, was thrown from the plane to the children who congregated below. In June, the Gates Flying Circus attracted thousands of Johnstowners to the airfield. The air team's stunts included wing-walking parachute jumping and gymnastic flying. More importantly, they gave thousands their first plane ride, free of charge. World War I changed the landscape of Westmont in other ways. Two years earlier, 241 Red Oak trees had been planted on Menoher Highway in memory of servicemen from the area who were buried on foreign soil. A brass marker was placed at the foot of each tree in memorial to each man. A fieldstone marker that read "Lest We Forget" placed on Petersons Plot.

In business affairs, Club Member John Waters was involved in a merger of major proportions, Waters, the president of National Radiator merged with Union Radiator. The $25,000,000 merger created the second largest manufacturer of radiators in the eastern United States. The corporate offices were based in Moxham and had offices and distribution facilities throughout the east coast. The company thrived as homes and larger buildings converted to steam heating systems. Waters was a strong presence at the Club and in the community.

With money in their pockets, both the wealthy and the mill workers could afford a variety of diversions. That summer, the New York Yankees with Lou Gehrig and Babe Ruth came to Johnstown. *The Johnstown Tribune* stated, " Ruth proved himself a genial fellow and was glad to shake the hand of every kid that got near him." Over 10,000 fans watched the Johnstown Johnnies defeat the Bronx Bombers at the Point Stadium. Afterwards the massive crowds had to be restrained by the Johnstown police.

Sunnehanna Country Club

Another major event in the country was the Gene Dempsey-George Tunney fight. Club member Philip Price, President of Johnstown Automobile Company, provided the Club with a twenty-five foot Atwater-Kent radio antenna to listen to the fight. In Johnstown, the Cambria and State Theaters were sold out, hundreds of folding chairs placed in the aisles, as men clamored to listen to the fight.

The community clamored to join the Club. The Club had 650 members, its largest membership that broke down to 393 active, 82 non-resident, and 89 social members. Johnstown continued to benefit from a strong national economy that continued to demand raw steel.

1929: The Best of Times, the Worst of Times

Sunnehanna Country Club had become what its founders had hoped for, the center of the social lives of the Club's members. The hiring of a full-time social hostess, further improved programs and member participation. Daily bridge parties were held. On Sunday evenings, a buffet dinner was introduced to furnish leisurely dinning.

Local organizations and businesses such as the Kiwanis, the local chapter of the American Institute of Banking, and Johnstown Automotive Club held large outings. Charles Schwab, the steel titan, was the featured speaker. Charitable functions also took place.

On July 17, 1929, the biggest event of the year occurred just outside the Club's grounds. Johnstown Municipal airport formally opened to great fanfare. The prior year, Camille Vinet, a former air mail pilot, was hired as the airport's pilot and instructor. Every evening he put his DeHaviland Moth Bi-Plane through a series of stunt maneuvers, delighting the crowds.

The dedication included David Ingals, assistant Secretary of the Navy; Charles Schwab, chairman of Bethlehem Steel; and famed aviatrix, Amelia Earhart. Day-long festivities started at 8:00 o'clock and ended after midnight. A sold-out lunch and dinner banquet for 450 celebrants was held at Sunnehanna where local dignitaries and the special guests spoke. For those who couldn't get a ticket, the speeches were carried on radio. The government

Johnstown's first airport. It ran alongside Sunnehanna's eleventh hole.

and the military had an interest in a growing airline industry; air technology would improve with greater domestic demand. Commercial aviators could also be a source for pilots in times of war. Amelia Earhart was the first to arrive. She left New York at 7:30 and arrived at 10:00, without needing a map. Army, Navy and Marine flyers performed aerial antics and stunts as 50,000 people watched from below. The day included a downtown parade, baseball game, fireworks, and finally, a street dance at the lower end of Main Street.

In the October of 1929, Wall Street collapsed under the weight of speculative loans used to buy stock. The markets collapse ended golf's "Golden Age". The specter of a changing economic environment did little to temper the enthusiasm of Sunnehanna Country Club's Board. President Michael Bracken's report to members extolled the increase in membership—more than 50 new members, and a doubling of income from golf and caddy fees. Bracken felt that continuing interest in the Club would permit all the debt to be retired in five years.

A New Reality

A year after Bracken's optimistic report, Sunnehanna Country Club's financial position had deteriorated significantly. The only specific mention of the nationally economic tragedy was made at the October 20, 1930 annual meeting: "The amount of sales for the year to date is $6,000 less than last year to date. This is largely accounted by a lack of parties due to the Depression." The Finance Committee stated, "Finances at Sunnehanna Country Club have not permitted yearly reduction of the outstanding 6%, 20-year Gold Bonds in accordance with the indenture. In fact the outlook is such that the Club has not been able to prepare a suitable plan for redeeming the bonds at maturity."

Travelers venturing to Johnstown from Ligonier would have been greeted by this billboard which used the Sunnehanna Clubhouse as a backdrop. The local dealership was owned by Ray Gardill, a Club member.

Sunnehanna Country Club

The Club managed to navigate the difficult environment in 1931, but also realized that a large number of resignations were likely. Rigid economy was used with all expenditures, but at year's end, the Club was $50,000 in debt. Nineteen thirty-one was a good year on the links for the Club's smoking members. The Liggett & Myers Tobacco Company awarded cigarettes in recognition of birdies; 14,000 free cigarettes were given to members.

Trophy Winners in Sunnehanna Women's Golf

1938

The Club instituted a series of austerity measures to avoid losing member's and to keep the doors opened. Golf professional, Bert Battel's salary was reduced from $150 per month to $100 and paid for eight months instead of nine. Battel was also told to "take fewer days off." To retain members, a moratorium was declared on delinquent member's accounts for six months and the Club announced it would operate on a cash basis.

To save members money, the $1 per-month cleaning bill was changed to a one-time charge of $8 per year. Caddie fees were cut from $1 to .75. The Club received .15 and the caddie .60. Guest green fees were cut to $2, except for Saturdays, Sundays, and holidays when it cost $3.

Finally, the Club cancelled further payments of interest on Sunnehanna Country Club bonds. The Board simply stated, "Financial conditions of the Club will not permit further payments."

As predicted, by years end the Club's membership dwindled from 378 members to 329 members. In the midst of the turbulent times, Mrs. J.K. Love made an untimely request of the Board; she asked that low-handicap woman be permitted to tee-off at anytime of day, any day. The Board's response was cool, "It was stated (at the meeting) that this would not be a good policy." Sunnehanna Country Club survived a difficult year; the same could not be said for other country clubs. While long-established clubs managed to survive, newer clubs founded by new money collapsed. Their youthful members were buried in debt as were the clubs they started. The use of gimmicks such as lifetime memberships, like at Sunnehanna, were used to attract upfront money further weakened the Club's ability to derive income.

In Johnstown, The Depression decimated the demand for steel and the community. In 1932, production of steel nationally was 25percent of what it was in 1929; 235 of 279 blast furnaces went unused. In the 1920's, Bethlehem Steel had reduced its work force in Johnstown by 7percent. The Depression exacerbated unemployment in the community. By 1934, 35percent of the community was looking for work. Bethlehem Steel's workforce stood at 8,500 men, down from 13,000 in 1923. The former grounds of

Johnstown Country Club were opened for community gardens to help people get by. These gardens remained in use through World War II. The Community Chest pleaded with the public for donations of mason jars so produce donated from local farmers could be canned.

Wilson Slick: The Right Man at the Right Time

Wilson Slick, center, enjoys a drink with his fellow members.

Wilson Slick's election in 1935 was a turning point for the Club. While dealing with the Club's current financial problems, he looked toward the future as well. One of the first steps was securing the services of Gene Sarazen and Olympic star Babe Didrickson to give a golf exhibition. Other professionals Helen Hicks Hass, the first major womans amateur to turn professional; Walter Hagan; Jimmy Thomson; Harry "Lighthorse" Cooper; Lawson Little, and Horton Smith followed.

Beginning in 1934, the Club embarked on a series of improvements. A caddy house and massive putting green were built. William Flynn, another of golf's finest architects, was hired to redesign the course. The clubhouse was almost entirely renovated. The condition of the clubhouse was deplorable. The overstuffed furniture, which had never been paid for, was held together by glue and string. Leaks were abundant as buckets were placed throughout the building to catch falling water. Nightly, tarpaulins were placed over the bowling alleys as water seeped through the open porch.

Sunnehanna Counry Club, 1936

There was no bar, and no Grille Room in 1934, at the end of his tenure there was.

Slick's dynamic leadership rehabilitated the Club physically, emotionally, and financially. On October 31, 1934 the Club had $1,551.59 in the bank: notes payable were $19,410, accounts payable $3,577.70, bonds payable $15,500 and accrued interest in the bonds $3,173. When he left office, the Club had outstanding debt of

Halloween Party, 1935

$3,000 and cash on hand of $3,000.

Slick's leadership also produced unintended consequences that benefited the Club and the community for years to come.

The Sunnehanna Invitational began in 1936. Other Club's ran similar events that proved to be financially successful. The Invitational increased membership use of the Club and improved the bottom line. The tournament also began a 68-year tradition of competitive amateur golf at Sunnehanna Country Club.

The exhibitions led to the building of Berkley Hills golf course, a municipal golf course. Equipment manufacturers preferred that professional players exhibit their skills at public facilities, free of charge to the spectator. The Local Works Division of the WPA allocated $36,140 to the project. The course opened in 1937.

A variety of other events and activities either began or were revived during Slick's seven-year tenure. Bowling was promoted as a winter activity in 1936. Another tradition that continues today started in 1937–the formal Black and White Ball.

New Challenges

World War II spurred renewed demand for steel and coal starting a boom that lasted into the 1950's. While the war ended the Depression and revived the local economy, it was still a hardship for Sunnehanna and other club across the country. The Club's male members were stretched across the globe serving in every arm of the military. While the Invitational wasn't held, the Club sponsored the Tri-State PGA tournament in 1942. In the finals, Ted Luther defeated Perry DelVecchio. The Club benefited financially as large crowds followed the finalists. The most surprising activity was the Calcutta auction pool that reached $2,500.

L-R: Julius Eckel, Patsy Grogan, Bud Griffith, Ralph Willet

Another public relations problem arose when the Club's operation was questioned during the war. Sacrifice was a national obsession. The press

Main Ballroom

constantly questioned the propriety of the Club operating at a time of war. The nation operated under a drastic ban on leisure driving. These restrictions forced clubs in rural areas to close during the war. Many never re-opened as the land was converted into homes for returning G.I.'s. The Club drastically curtailed staff and elected to close every Monday. It also opened the course to soldiers on leave, permitting them to play the course free of charge.

Only ordinary maintenance could be done, work on improving the Grill Room was suspended by the War Production Board officials. Golf adapted to the restrictive environment. Suspending its championships, the USGA advocated clubs utilize unused sections of their properties for Victory Gardens, Sunnehanna did not adopt this idea. However, golf balls were highly prized. New balls were rare during the war; rubber was needed for more important purposes. The only option was recycled balls. A young caddy from Brownstown, Bob Hahn, recalled, "This guy I was caddying for hit his ball in the woods on eight. He told me not to come out till I found it. He walked off with his clubs. I eventually found it and joined him on the fifteenth hole." Sunnehanna Country Club's survival through the Depression and World War II was no small feat. From 1932 through 1952, 200 new clubs opened, and 600 disappeared.

1950 Signs reads Joinng the Suffragettes. They worry about Starting Times. DOWN WITH GENTS!

The 50's and 60's

With the War's end came the post-war prosperity of the fifties. It was a time of unparalleled growth. Sunnehanna Country Club thrived and planned for the future. The clubhouse underwent the first of many modernizations. An aggressive tree planting program on the golf course began under Howard

Picking. The lives of the Club's members and their families revolved around the Club. Days were spent playing golf, swimming and, especially on weekends, dinner at the day's end. Bowling leagues formally began in 1946 and attracted strong participation. Teams like Willet's Well Builts, Replogles Flood Frees, Quaker Sales Black Tops and the Bethlehem Iron Men competed in a league every Saturday.

Julius Eckel won numerous bowling titles. An enthusiastic member, he was responsible for Sunnehanna's monthly newsletter for many years.

Sunnehanna Country Club

One tradition ended and another began in the fifties as the Sunnehanna Invitational was terminated after 1951. The Calcutta was compromised by professional gamblers in Johnstown. Rather than sacrifice the Club's reputation, the popular tournament was ended. Five years later, Charles Kunkle, who successfully competed against the best amateur golfers in the country, sought to bring tournament golf back to Sunnehanna. He proposed a stroke play tournament free of a calcutta. A motion was made and the Sunnehanna Amateur began in 1956. The Club's financial condition had never been better. At year's end in 1956, the Club had 550 members, in 1951 membership stood at 363.

In the fifties and sixties the makeup of the Club underwent significant change. The biggest change was the membership. Previously restricted to a small group of people, predominantly Bethlehem Steel and Mines' upper management, suppliers to the steel company, and various business leaders and professionals, the Club gradually opened its doors. It was the centerpiece for the finest social and community functions in Johnstown.

Wayne Wolfe, Charles Kunkle, and Doctor George Wheeling with the Wheeling trophy

The Sunnehanna Amateur quickly became one of the best amateur tournaments in the country. While the competition was important, members also looked forward to the entertainment. Nightly, the big band sounds of Tommy Dorsey, Count Basie and The Glenn Miller Band filled the corridors and ballroom. Lionel Hampton, The Mills Brothers, and The Lennox Sisters performed to a packed house. By the end of three days, members collapsed from the late nights.

Jeanne Rose and Dorothy Kunkle

With the success of the Sunnehanna Amateur, Dr. George Wheeling, a strong supporter golf and a civic leader, started a high school golf tournament to promote and improve high school golf in the area. Beginning with four teams, the tournament grew to as many as 19 teams and is a highlight of the scholastic season. Today, the George F. Wheeling Athletic and Educational Trust Scholastic Tournament continues to run the tournament and also provides five scholarships to several local colleges for deserving students.

In the late sixties, two individuals took charge of the junior golf program and influenced the lives of thousands of children. Dorothy Kunkle and Jeanne Rose assumed responsibility for the junior golf program and gave guidance, discipline, and encouragement to kids of all ages and abilities. Under their leadership, and Head Professional John Goettlicher's support, junior golf thrived. Modest restrictions on play provided summertime days of endless golf. The result: the Pennsylvania's top junior program. Players succeeded at the highest levels of competition winning the West Penn Junior, Pennsylvania State Junior, and on the national stage, qualifying for the U.S. Junior. No two people positively affected the lives of more people than Dorothy Kunkle and Jeanne Rose. Their remarkable, unselfish dedication continued for more than thirty years.

The Seventies and the End of Steel

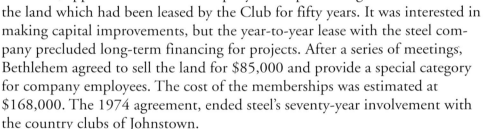

Robert G. Rose

The seventies were a time of great change. The nation struggled with divisions at home. In Johnstown, the first indications of the impending collapse of the domestic steel industry appeared. Bethlehem Steel gave notice that it planned to slash production of ingot steel by almost 60percent over the next four years. Employment was cut by almost 45percent. With this backdrop, Robert Rose, Club President, approached the steel company about purchasing the land which had been leased by the Club for fifty years. It was interested in making capital improvements, but the year-to-year lease with the steel company precluded long-term financing for projects. After a series of meetings, Bethlehem agreed to sell the land for $85,000 and provide a special category for company employees. The cost of the memberships was estimated at $168,000. The 1974 agreement, ended steel's seventy-year involvement with the country clubs of Johnstown.

Howard Picking and Ronald Reagan at Sunnehanna Country Club.

Free to make decisions on its future Sunnehanna Country Club engaged in a variety of improvements. In 1981, the expansion of the clubhouse eliminated the circle that went around the golf course and the putting green. To make up for lost parking, the eighteenth green was torn up. Additional locker rooms sadly ended bowling and removed an important piece of history: eight foot murals of community life that graced the walls were lost in the renovation. Today, renovations are under way to return some of the clubhouses original lines and beauty. One thing didn't change: membership's devotion to the principles that founded the Club.

After eighty years, Sunnehanna Country Club stands as a testament to an earlier age. The catalyst for the Club— steel and coal—are no longer apart of the economic life of the community. The demise of steel making in Johnstown changed Sunnehanna and the community. Sunnehanna adapted to a new world and moved forward. With time, the membership has become more diverse and represents a broader cross-section of Johnstown. But one principle remains from its earliest beginnings, an oasis for golf and social activities that match anything found in a larger community with views that are unequaled.

HENRY M. ROGERS
Clubhouse Architect

Just as Sunnehanna's golf course was designed by world-class architect A. W. Tillinghast, its Clubhouse was by an equally skilled and prolific, but unheralded architect, Henry M. Rogers. Henry M. Rogers was a worldly man who came of age in Johnstown at the height of the City's industrial boom. From the Roaring 20's into the 1960's, Rogers was at the forefront of both commercial and residential construction in Johnstown. Henry M. Rogers was the central architect of his time in Johnstown and those structures are now magnificent landmarks to his genius. The Sunnehanna Clubhouse was designed by Rogers to be the showcase of Johnstown society and its understated elegance was a reflection of his understanding of matching a timeless golf course with a lasting Clubhouse.

Although Henry M. Rogers' architectural legacy is abundantly evident in the many buildings and homes standing testament in Johnstown, his life and times reflect a hard working, private, family man. As his grandson Phil Newbaker recalled, "Grandfather was ever the inventor, happy in his craft and his life, which helped him in the creative process. I well remember Grandfather drafting cartoons to spice up the lives of his family and he was well ahead of his time in the characters, content and message of his cartoons." Newbaker carries on the family mantle by assisting owners of Rogers' homes-custom mill replacement features for his Grandfather's designs from the rambling confines of the Johnstown Planning Mill. Remarkably,

Newbaker recovered and has been the caretaker of architectural plans for many of Rogers' Johnstown creations, including homes originally designed for the giants of commerce such as Love, Waters, Replogle, Fronheiser and Thackray. These plans are works of art that are true museum pieces rarely seen in contemporary home design.

In researching the biography of Henry M. Rogers, Newbaker led me up the back steps of his lumber mill and provided me a glimpse of the tireless scholar that Rogers was as we prowled through his "filing cabinet" (a 6' x 8' vault) that contained clippings from *Architectural Digest* for twenty-five years that related to golf course Clubhouses. Newport, The Country Club, Skokie, Philadelphia Cricket, National Golf Links of America, Oakmont and Sleepy Hollow were just a few of the hundreds of pictures and plans that

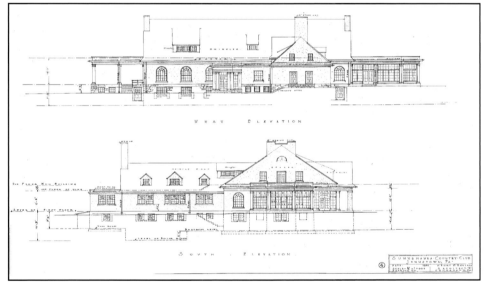

Rogers drew upon to design Sunnehanna's Clubhouse. When I related to Newbaker the parallels between the Shinnecock Hills Clubhouse and Sunnehanna, the description immediately registered and we dug and dug to find Stanford White's plans that no doubt inspired Henry M. Rogers. We did not locate those plans and pictures, but knowing the far-reaching influences which inspired Rogers, we can be sure that the stately and elegant clubhouse that opened in 1923 at Sunnehanna was uniquely a Henry M. Rogers design, as well as a "blueprint" for the transition of American architecture to a new, genuine, understated and timeless expression of style.

By George Wolfe

Bethlehem Steel

*F*or its first fifty years, Sunnehanna was directly tied to Bethlehem Steel's appreciation and propagation of the game of golf. Charles Schwab, the first President of Bethlehem Steel, was a Member of Sunnehanna. Eugene Grace, Bethlehem Steel's Chairman for 40 years, was responsible for the steel company's contribution to Sunnehanna, Saucon Valley, Sparrows Point, Bethlehem Golf Club, Silver Lake and the engagement of architects such as A. W. Tillinghast, Herbert Strong, Perry Maxwell, Donald Ross and William O. Gordon. The golfing culture that was intertwined with Bethlehem Steel will be described in these pages, but research revealed that Bethlehem's predecessor in Johnstown, Cambria Iron Company, also had an appreciation for golf. In point of fact, Sunnehanna is really celebrating its 103rd Birthday as a golf course has existed in the Borough of Westmont since 1900. Again, research showed direct and uninterrupted ties from Sunnehanna to a turn-of-the-century course constructed a mere driver and eight iron from Sunnehanna's fourteenth tee.

The significance of having a company such as Bethlehem Steel interested in golf is demonstrated by the corporation's former status in the business world. In addition to its headquarters in its namesake city, the company owned plants in Johnstown, Pottstown, Steelton, Lebanon, Williamsport, Lackawanna, Baltimore, Buffalo, Burns Harbor, Los Angeles, San Francisco and Seattle. Bethlehem Steel was responsible for the prominent buildings, bridges and skyscrapers in boom time America, including the George Washington Bridge and Chrysler Building in New York, the Ben Franklin Bridge in Philadelphia and the Golden Gate Bridge in San Francisco. In 1959, Bethlehem Steel had six names in *Business Week* magazine's list of highest paid executives, with Chairman Arthur B. Homer being the highest paid executive in the United States. In Johnstown, Bethlehem Steel permeated every segment of the city. Employing 16,000 people for decades at a stretch, Bethlehem and the businesses that served it were the bedrock of the Johnstown economy. Naturally, Bethlehem's cultural commitment to golf and recreation is the central reason Sunnehanna was created and sustained. Also, the Bethlehem Management Club, Bethco Pines and the Bethco Rod and Gun Club all promoted the pastoral life far removed from the wheels of steel making. In short, the Bethlehem Steel legacy lives on in the magnificent form of Sunnehanna Country Club.

By George Wolfe

Bert Battel
Sunnehanna's First Professional

Bert Battel, Sunnehanna's first Head Professional came to Johnstown in 1920 from Flushing Country Club in Queens, New York. At the age of 14, he apprenticed under the tutelage of Jack White, the 1904 British Open champion, at the prestigious Sunningdale Golf Club in Surrey, England. As a young assistant, he dealt with the political and business elite of England. In a remarkable story, he became the regular golf partner with one of the greatest leaders of the 20th century, Winston Churchill. Churchill, a fervent golfer in his early days when time permitted, phoned Sunningdale for a round of golf. The young Battel was his companion that day and every Sunday thereafter.

He traveled across the Atlantic in 1913. Golf's explosive growth in America created endless professional openings that were filled mostly by professionals from Scotland and England. Battel found employment in Queens and within months sent word to his hometown sweetheart, Margaret Chastel, to join him in America. Bert met her on the docks of New York and they promptly got married.

In January of 1916, Bert Battell was a part of a historic meeting in New York City. The gathering at the Taplow Club in the Hotel Martinique was attended by, among others, Walter Hagan and A.W. Tillinghast, and consisted of leading amateurs and head professionals. The meeting led to the establishment of the PGA of America and Bert Battell was one of the organization's 35 founding professional members.

Seven years later, Battel was hired as Head Professional at Cambria Country Club. His responsibilities included teaching the Club's growing membership the royal and ancient game, organizing events and maintaining the grounds; his salary $125 a month. Battell's most coveted skills were as a club maker. Every club from his hands was made to the specific requirements of the golfer. Battel made hundreds of sets of club throughout his career. Prized by golf collectors in Johnstown, his putters are still used by golfers in the area.

Battell was also a fine player, and repeatedly established new course records. Late in 1934, he made the national sports pages. In a single day at Sunnehanna, he shot 66 then 64, which established a new course record. Two years later, in Sunnehanna's second exhibition, he defeated legendary golfer Walter Hagan by two strokes shooting even par 70.

In 1937, Bert Battell moved on to North Fork Country Club and a year later, to the brand new Berkley Hills Golf Course, a public golf facility. There Battel influenced a new generation of professionals. One youngster who, along with his friends, repeatedly tried to sneak on the course was John Goettlicher. Living next to the course, Berkley Hills became a second home for he and his brother, Rudy. Not old enough to caddy, Battel asked the youngster if he wanted to clean clubs. It was an offer that changed a life. Several years later Battel encouraged John Goettlicher to become a head professional.

Years later, John Goettlicher moved from Head Professional at Berkley Hills to Sunehanna Country Club. Bert Battel came to America for opportunity and a better life and gave the same to others.

L-R: Henry Schneck, Pro, Berkley Hills G.C.; Wilson Slick, President, Sunnehanna CC; George Anderson Professional, North Ford CC; Bert Battel; Bob Gutwein, Professional, Sunnehanna CC.

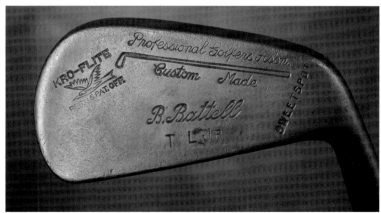

Hand-made golf club

Sunnehanna's Golf Course
An Unmatched Pedigree

At Sunnehanna's Board of Governors meeting on February 18 1921, Grounds Committee chairman H. A. Berg was instructed to secure the talents of a "golf course expert" to examine the grounds for the proposed course and provide an estimated cost of construction. Bert Battel, the clubs golf professional, aided Berg recommending Albert Warren Tillinghast, recognized nationally as one of the finest architects in golf. Battel first met Tillinghast at a gathering of leading amateurs and 35 professional golfers at the Hotel Martinique in New York City. The meeting on January 16, 1916 led to the formation of the PGA of America.

Tillinghast Gets to Work

Albert Warren Tillinghast

Tillinghast's first commission was Shawnee-on-the-Delaware in eastern Pennsylvania. Opened in 1911, Tillinghast's initial foray into golf course design was well received. At Pine Valley, Tillinghast lent his advice and he contributed to two of the courses most revered holes: the par-five seventh and the difficult thirteenth. Additional successes followed at San Francisco Golf Club and Somerset Hills. His varied designs and original approaches as to each course quickly established him as one of the nation's finest architects. Baltusrol hired him in 1918 to design a second course. Instead, he recommended tearing up the original and built two championship courses: the Lower and Upper. In 1921, Tillinghast was commissioned to build two courses in Mamaroneck, New York. Winged Foot's East and West course opened in 1923.

By early April 1921, A.W. Tillinghast's services were contracted, as well as his head of construction Mr. Honeyman, who was responsible for converting Tillinghast's vision into reality. Tillinghast, while discussing a proposal for the new Erie Golf Club, stated on April 6, 1921:

> *My head of construction has been retained by clubs at Williamsport and Johnstown (Pa) and I will be able to allow him to visit your course from time to time. His instructions will mean a great deal to you and while I do not urge his retention because of any great profit to myself, I do urge it because I know it will save you a great deal of money in the end.*

Later in April, Tillinghast was putting stakes in the ground for the proposed course. Surrounded by unsurpassed views of the Allegheny Mountains, Tillinghast envisioned the course meandering 360 degrees around a possible location for the clubhouse. While mapping out the course he gave instructions for the ground to be tilled and limed.

The Golf Course

Architects typically provided their employers no more than a one or two days on site. The demand for their services outstripped the available time. Days were required to travel to proposed sites. This was the "Golden Age" of American golf course architecture as national economic prosperity drove demand for new courses across the country. In 1916, there were 742 golf courses many rudimentary, like Johnstown Country Club and designed for newcomers to the game. When Sunnehanna opened in 1923 there were 1,903 courses by 1929 the number of courses would explode to 5,648.

In some cases architects used only topographical maps to diagram a course, never visiting the location. Unlike other fellow architects, Tillinghast did go to the site and inspect the land. He would then prepare an outline of the course and sketch or diagram holes.

Equally important to the architect's success was an experienced construction supervisor and work crew. Unfortunately, many courses were built with local labor. Usually recent emigrants, the final result was a course that differed greatly from the architect plan. The preferable method was employed at Sunnehanna. Tillinghast's chief of construction oversaw the work with Tillinghast periodically revisiting the site to make needed changes.

SUNNEHANNA CLUB TO REVIEW PLANS

Noted Golf Course Architect to Speak at Chamber of Commerce Tonight

A. W. Tillinghast, noted golf course architect, who has been retained by the Sunnehanna Country Club for the construction of the proposed 18-hole course on the new site of the club in Upper Yoder Township, is in Johnstown today in conference with officials of the local club. This evening he will address a meeting of the club members in the Chamber of Commerce headquarters, when he will explain the plans already drawn for the new golf course. It is expected that all members of the club who can possibly arrange to do so will be in attendance.

Tonight's meeting is of utmost importance to the members of Sunnehanna Country Club, in that it affords an opportunity for each man interested in golf to express his personal views on all problems concerning the laying out of the course. Any suggestion for improvement of the plans, it is announced, will be given careful consideration and where deemed advisable under local conditions will be adopted and incorporated into the general layout of the course.

Mr. Tillinghast has planned many of the country's best golf courses and he is held as one of the country's greatest authorities on matters of this nature.

Financial Note.
From Life.
Marriage is a love bond; divorce is a liberty bond.

His initial work done, Tillinghast addressed Sunnehanna's members on June 1, 1921 unveiling his proposed layout for the first time. The Johnstown Tribune noted that Tillinghast had already designed many of the nation's finest courses and stated, "He is held as one of the country's greatest authorities on matters of this nature."

The Board met again with Tillinghast and Henry Rogers, the eventual clubhouse architect, on September 7. Tillinghast reported significant progress in five months with 11 greens completed at a cost of $9,500, not including seeding. The Board was provided a revised cost estimate for construction, between $30,000 and $40,000, considerably less than the original estimate of $60,000 to $70,000.

A possible reason for the substantially lower construction costs might be explained in the photo and corresponding ad. The green at Essex Country Club in West Orange, New Jersey, was built in 1917 and was used in an advertisement to promote a catalog for plastic models of greens designed by the renowned architect. The green is almost an exact replica of the thirteenth green at Sunnehanna. Unfortunately, Tillinghast's catalog has never been found, so only assumptions can be made. To save time and money, golf course architects frequently used similar ideas on other courses. Comparable versions of holes at Sunnehanna are found at other Tillinghast designed courses. The concept of building greens using models without hiring an architect was new and revolutionary.

Another possible reason for the lower cost could have been the use of labor provided by Cambria Steel. Omnipresent in Johnstown, Cambria Steel and its predecessor, Bethlehem Steel, provided generous support to Sunnehanna, including company workers, but again no specific information is available.

Essex County Country Club's eleventh, 1917   *Sunnehanna's thirteenth, the flared back edges are currently rough.*

The Golf Course

One Year Later

A first year's progress report was provided to the Board on January 12, 1922 with the commensurate costs associated with the work finished in 1921:

17 Greens completed and 55 Greenside Bunkers complete	$9385.06
8 Fairway Bunkers complete	$1600.00
14,185 Yards of Sod Cut, Handled, and Laid	$897.65
Planting of 68 Trees	$246.50
Clearing of Woods on Numbers 2, 8, and 10 Fairways	$802.31
Picking Stone and Staking Fairway	$27.00
Fees to Tillinghast and Honeyman	$4365.41
Seeds, Tools etc.	$4386.69
Compost	$411.00
Total	**$22,701.62**

The next year, A.W. Tillinghast and Sunnehanna Country Club parted ways. Tillinghast was a man of tremendous ego and poor temperament, made worse by a propensity to drink in excess. He frequently alienated his employers with his boorish behavior; Sunnehanna, apparently, was no exception. J.H. McGovern completed Tillinghast's plan, overseeing the work on the course and at the same time; the construction of the clubhouse.

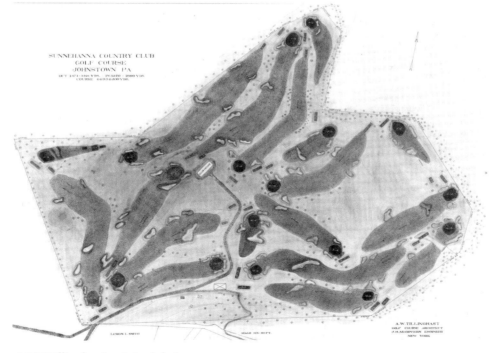

A.W. Tillinghast's original design map

The Golf Course

In September of 1923, Sunnehanna Country Club opened but only sixteen holes were deemed ready for play.

Open for Play

Less than three years after the course opened for play, the members were summoned to a meeting at the behest of the Golf and Grounds Committee. The use of an inexperienced work crew after firing Tillinghast and his construction company resulted in numerous turf problems. Dissatisfied with the slow maturation of the course, the committee believed changes were needed for the course to reach its full potential. The fairways struggled to grow quality turf. Poor soil, described as "shaly in nature", precluded the ground from holding moisture and permitting quality turf to grow. M.J. Bracken, Committee Chairman, was anxious to proceed with the project. At the meeting, he announced that top dressing and trucks to deliver it were secured, free of charge. The consensus of the attendees was that the growing popularity of golf and the course's potential justified solving the problem and the commensurate capital expenditure. All they needed was to hire someone with the background and ability to resolve the ongoing problems at Sunnehanna. That person was found 75 miles to the west of Johnstown.

Emil Loeffler: Problem Solver

"Johnstown will in a few years be known all over the eastern part of the United States as having one of the best constructed and located course in the region", opined Emil Loeffler, superintendent at Oakmont Country Club after viewing Sunnehanna for the first time. Loeffler and John McGlynn, who Loeffler succeeded as superintendent at Oakmont in 1916, were business partners in a golf course consulting and design business. Nationally known because of the exquisite condition of the renowned Pittsburgh course, securing the services of Loeffler was greeted with great enthusiasm by the Board and the members.

No one in the history of golf in Western Pennsylvania can come close to Emil Loeffler's remarkable combination of skills. In 1927, Loeffler was named Head Professional at Oakmont and continued as Course Superintendent,

Emil Loeffler points to work being done.

36

The Golf Course

holding both positions until 1946. An outstanding player, he won the Pennsylvania State Open in 1920 and 1922 and the West Penn Open in 1920. As a teacher, he worked with Western Pennsylvania's best players and is credited with sharpening the skills of Sam Parks, who won the 1935 US Open at Oakmont. He also found time to design over twenty golf courses.

Beginning in August of 1926, Loeffler drove from Pittsburgh every Saturday personally supervising the reconstruction of the fairways and the greens. Interviewed on one of his visits, Loeffler heaped praise on the course:

> "You people in Johnstown have a great golf course within 20 minutes of the city and with a location and natural beauty that is unexcelled anywhere. The soil is in better shape than when we started the famous Oakmont course and the general layout here offers far greater possibilities for a great course. I predict within a few years Johnstown will have visitors coming just for the opportunity to play this course."

Loeffler believed that with a little harrowing of the ground and the generous use of fertilizer, the soil could support excellent turf and result in a spectacular golf course. Two members of his staff worked permanently on site, one in charge of seeding the other fertilizer. Grounds chairman Bracken

Aerial of Sunnehanna in 1929. The thirteenth green, front foreground, with a boomerang bunker that served as fairway bunker for the fifteenth hole. Boomerang bunkers can also be found on four (right center) and on sixteen (far left center.) Boomerang bunkers were often found on Tillinghast designs.

and his assistant John Cook reviewed and personally supervised the work daily. By October, all but two of the fairways were completed and the grass sown.

The course reconditioning was a great success and Emil Loeffler was hired to annually review the course. His reports gave advice ranging from changes in tees, bunkers, greens, turf quality, and overall maintenance.

In retrospect, some changes could be considered mistakes. In 1929, Superintendent Walter Anderson was instructed to remove fairway bunkers on fifteen as well as the Sahara of sand that existed in the third fairway, turning both into grass bunkers.

The fifteenth hole, a double-dogleg par five, featured a boomerang bunker off the tee that served as a greenside bunker for the thirteenth hole. A cross bunker made players pause when contemplating their second shot. Sixty-five yards wide, the cross bunker dissected the fairway and was utilized by Tillinghast on many of his finest courses.

Sunnehanna was originally an inland links course. Player's shots were played close to the ground over the rolling topography. Trees rarely impeded play. Built prior to the advent of central watering systems, players were provided generous openings to the green encouraging bump-and-run golf. Misplayed shots careened into deep, yawning bunkers.

The Worst of Times

The final collapse of the stock market in October 1929 changed country club's goals from growth to survival. The Depression and subsequent decline in memberships eviscerated club's balance sheets. Golf course budgets were slashed. Bunkers were eliminated because of the associated cost of sand and maintenance. Greens shrunk in size to save gas. Members occasionally took over basic chores like cutting greens, fairways and tees, and raking bunkers.

Sunnehanna persevered in the early years of the Depression. In fact, the courses condition improved because of Loeffler's guidance. It was to be short lived.

In 1931, Loeffler hailed the course's progress: "You have the best turf I have ever seen. Your greens are 50% better than the Pittsburgh Field Club. In another year, you can handle any tournament here, the only thing you need is more sand in the traps." Loeffler recommended moving or enlarging tees and building a new green on number eight, but economic conditions made any changes impractical.

A year later, the Club had fallen into desperate financial condition, and eliminated Loeffler's annual inspection saving $50. The Board determined that seven men would work nine hours a day on the course rather than ten men, working ten hours a day. Grounds crew wages were slashed from $.40 to $.35 per hour, the mechanics salary cut from $.45 to $.40 per hour.

Two weeks later, the Board realized the wage cuts were insufficient and implemented a sliding pay scale. Workers pay began at $.35 per hour until April 10, $.30 per hour until July 1, then $.27 per hour for the rest of the year. Weed pickers, who physically removed dandelions from the greens and fairways, were paid $.15 per hour.

Building for the Future

The nation was still griped by economic hardship when the Club's members supported, through voluntary contributions, the building of a caddie house and practice green in 1934. Both were the ideas of Cecil C. McClain, chairman of the Club's Tournament Committee. McClain felt the additions were needed to keep the club's facilities in step with its big city brethren.

In spite of a caddie strike that had entered its second summer, the caddie house opened in July of 1934. Built at a cost of $1200, the building was designed and built by club member William L. Carstensen. Constructed with native fieldstone with a large fireplace inside, it had a

Snapshots of Sunnehanna Club's New Golf Property

Club members dedicate new putting-pitching green.

Special Dedication Committee (left to right) —C. C. McLain, E. W. Trexler (chairman), M. J. McCleary, John W. Cook, W. A. Reiber and Mrs. L. R. Owen. George J. Hahn and B. T. Mahaffey were other members of the committee.

capacity for 100 caddies. The building stood behind the first tee and eventually became the pro shop.

The green, opened for use in August of 1935, cost $400 to build. Designed by H. Burton Musser from The Pennsylvania State University, the green was declared to exceed anything found at the finest metropolitan courses in the country in terms of beauty and function.

Musser, a pioneer in golf course agronomy, taught at Pennsylvania State University for 37 years. He sponsored the first Greenkeeper conference in 1934 entitled "Better Turf Grasses". Musser also published the first comprehensive book on golf course turf management through the auspices of the United States Golf Association.

Seeded with south German bent-grass, the green abutted the caddie house and was 12,000 square feet; 10,000 used for putting and 2,000 for chipping. The work was overseen by course superintendent Calvin Stutzman and done entirely by his staff. Three thousand cubic yards of soil was moved to build the green. The willingness to take on these projects signaled the club's determination to build for the future in spite of the vicissitudes of the time.

Aerial view in 1936 before William Flynn did work. Twelfth green top right has no front right bunker.

William Flynn and a New Course

Buoyed by the enthusiastic response to the putting green, the Board contemplated improving the course. William Flynn, another famed Philadelphia architect, was retained to review the course and provide a cost estimate for his proposal.

Flynn had earned a formidable reputation from many of his designs. The best known was his redesign of Shinnecock Hills in Southampton, New York. Another notable success was Cherry Hills in Denver, Colorado.

The Golf Course

William Flynn's work as a golf course architect assured his place in golf history. Flynn was responsible championship courses at The Cascades at the Homestead, and Glen View Club. He was especially prolific in Pennsylvania providing stylish designs at Lancaster Country Club and Philadelphia Country Club, to name a few. Interestingly, Flynn's work at Sunnehanna was unknown until research on this book was undertaken. The combination of a Tillinghast original design and a Flynn

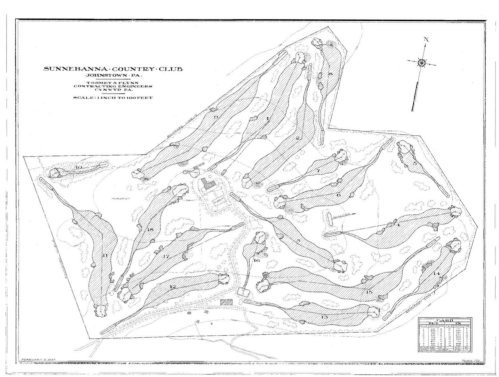

William Flynn's proposal for Sunnehanna Country Club Feb 2, 1937

redesign is unprecedented. Other prominent redesigns by Flynn include Merion and The Country Club in Brookline, Massachusetts; both have hosted American golf's major championship.

Flynn's involvement in golf can be traced to his youth competing against amateur star Francis Ouimet. After his tenure as greens superintendent at Merion and military service in World War I, Flynn joined Howard Toomey and formed a successful partnership. While business thrived, Flynn, a former professional tennis player and owner of the Philadelphia Eagles, remained committed to his roots conducting revolutionary turf grass research. He also was a guest lecturer at The Pennsylvania State University on agronomy and greenskeeping.

At the annual meeting in October 1936, the Board confidently announced to the members, "We hope to report considerable progress within a very short time; a modern 1937 golf course is the objective."

Flynn's proposal was estimated to cost $32,749. The Club hired John McGlynn as superintendent architect. McGlynn was familiar with Sunnehanna, the result of his partnership with Emil Loeffler. The former Greenskeeper at Oakmont was hired on a pay-as-you-go basis for $25 per day.

The initial work was financed with the profits from three sources over the prior four years: green fees, the Sunnehanna Invitational, and the Exhibitions amounting to $8,800. Work began mid-summer 1938, and changes were made to six holes. The improvements ended when Club President Wilson Slick and the Board refused to raise dues for the upcoming year, electing to focus capital expenditures on the clubhouse. With no money

Aerial after William Flynn worked on course. The twelfth hole (foreground center) now has a greeenside bunker. Across the road the sixteenth hole has a massive waste area. Another addition of note was the large waste area on the ninth hole (top left along treeline).

available for the course, several longtime members of the greens committee resigned in disgust.

Some changes were later eliminated, but a few changes by Flynn remain integral parts of the course. The most easily noticeable addition is the mound and bunker to the left of the second green. Flynn proposed this type of bunkering throughout his plan.

The original second green sloped dramatically from back-to-front with a second steep tier in the back right of the green. Players of modest ability watched putts from above the hole quickly gather speed and travel off the green and down the fairway. The new green remained challenging but the severe slope was reduced, the back tier removed.

The other major change was the twelfth hole. The raised square green was reduced in size and an additional front right bunker added to toughen the approach shot.

William Flynn

The Second World War

Having survived the Depression, the Club and the golf course soon faced new obstacles with the Second World War. Reduced revenues because of the war again affected the Club's bottom lines and reduced maintenance budgets. Because of rationing, Sunnehanna had difficulty acquiring fuel and fertilizer to maintain the course. To make up for gas shortages greens were reduced in size, some substantially.

Keeping the course opened for play during the war was an achievement. Many courses in rural or isolated areas partially or totally closed for the duration of the war.

An even bigger problem was labor shortages. Sunnehanna's Grounds Committee attributed the shoddy condition of the bunkers due to a scarcity of labor. Changes were made to the course to save on maintenance. The cross-bunker on the thirteenth hole was filled. The boomerang bunker that served as a greenside bunker on thirteen and fairway bunker on fifteen was reduced to just a greenside bunker

Wages, substantially reduced during the Depression, were adjusted to hopefully find competent help. A skeleton crew worked on the course and adhered to a strict budget. The budget for 1945 approved hiring only four men to work for eight months, 30 days a month. One other man was hired to work four months. They were paid $.65 per hour. Four men were hired to pick weeds for five weeks at $.45 per hour.

Post War: Trees and Constant Change

After almost 17 years of hardship in the post war era, golfers looked forward to better days and the Club's Grounds Committee planned for the future.

Beginning in 1949, Sunnehanna commenced an aggressive tree planting program. Thousands of trees, primarily pines, were planted on the course. Influenced by parkland courses cut out of heavily wooded land, courses devoid of trees were converted by members that wanted a softer appearance during their rounds.

In hindsight, the decision to plant thousands of pine trees could be considered a mistake. Previously, elm trees were the predominant tree on many early courses. It was the perfect tree for golf courses. The elms deep roots, arched branches, and canopy permitted air flow and speckled sunlight. Its shape also permitted errant shots to be played under its limbs. Over forty elm trees were planted when Sunnehanna was built and more in 1932, only a few survive today. Sadly, Dutch Elm Disease eliminated these trees from golf courses and street boulevards throughout America.

In response, clubs went on unruly tree planting binges that were not well thought out. As the trees matured, they substantially reduced sunlight and airflow and resulted in various diseases and funguses, particularly on greens. Sunnehanna's reliance on mostly pine trees created these problems and eliminated original shot values. The worst outcome was undoubtedly the elimination of the spectacular views afforded golfers when the course opened.

Aerial in 1957. Small pine trees dot the course.

The Golf Course

The Club's first watering system was installed in 1954. First proposed in 1948 by Toomey and Flynn Construction, it provided water for greens and tees only. While the watering system was being installed, the Grounds Committee added bunkers on 14 holes.

The Influence of Tournament Golf

Before the war, new tees were built for the Invitational contestants on the fourth, eighth and eighteenth holes to toughen the course. With the Invitational's return in 1946, the sixth and eleventh holes were converted to par fives.

Ten years later, responding to the success of the Sunnehanna Amateur, new tees were added on the second, fourth, sixth, seventh, fourteenth, and seventeenth holes in 1956. The course was lengthened by over 150 yards with the new tees. Trees were planted everywhere and bunkers were added to tighten the course for amateur golf's best players.

The most notable change was about to come.

William Gordon and the Eighth Hole

In 1957 work began on a new eighth hole. The original hole, a modest 285 yard par four, encouraged shots to be played over a gaping bunker to a tiny green. Players on the second tee frequently ducked as the word "Fore" emanated from the eighth tee. First proposed by Emil Loeffler in 1931, the Club was financially fit and prepared to finally change the direction of the hole and build a new green.

William F. Gordon was hired to design the hole. A few members of Sunnehanna were familiar with Gordon because of his work on several Bethlehem Steel affiliated courses, particularly Saucon Valley in Bethlehem, Pennsylvania. Gordon designed the Grace course and redesigned Perry Maxwell's original layout of the Old Course. He was also responsible Saucon Valley's third course, Weyhill, built in 1967.

William Gordon, right, partnered with his son David, left, beginning in 1952.

As a superintendent for the golf course division of Peterson Seed Company, Gordon supervised projects for Willie Park Jr., Donald Ross and Devereux Emmet, the best architects in the history of the game. In 1923, he joined the firm of Toomey and Flynn (note correspondence from William Flynn on page 41) where he remained until 1941. Sunnehanna called upon

The Golf Course

Bobby Clampett tees-off in 1980.

William Gordon for advice on many issues because of his background and extreme knowledge.

Used for the first time in the 1959 Sunnehanna Amateur, the new eighth hole was substantially more difficult. The average score was almost a half stroke higher than the previous year. The drive intimidated the best players in golf. The tree lined hole required a drive of 200 yards to carry an overgrown gully, nicknamed "Devil's Gulch". The green was moved fifty yards to the right of the original eighth green. Surrounded by oak trees and bunkers, it was a substantially more difficult hole from tee-to-green. No hole has determined the eventual winner of the Sunnehanna Amateur more than the eighth.

The eighth hole in the fall of 2003. Bunkers across the face of the hill were built in 1999.

The Golf Course

In 1960, par was reduced from 72 to 70 as the sixth hole changed to a par four and the fourteenth hole converted from a 297-yard par four to a 250- yard par three from the back tees.

The same year, a new watering system for the entire course was installed. William Gordon was hired again. Estimates for the project were between $65,000 and $75,000. When contracts were finally awarded, the cost was $84,296, not including architects fees of $7,220.

A massive water hazard was added to serve as holding ponds for the system. The water hazard stretched from the left side of fourteenth fairway to in front of the fifteenth tee. Then it meandered across the fourth fairway and continued along the fourth green and most of the length of the fifth hole.

When the project was done, the fifth hole was dramatically changed, raising the tee 12 feet. The championship tee was also moved 30 yards right of its previous location.

Problems were evident immediately. The ponds liners failed, water spilled into the coal mine shafts that ran underneath the hillside. The result was a muddy mess, which eventually led to abandoning most of the hazard.

The Seventy's and Eighty's

The ever evolving Sunnehanna golf course faced few major changes in the sixties and seventies. In 1981 as apart of an overall clubhouse improvement project, the circle around the clubhouse was closed. The lost parking was resolved with the elimination of the putting green and the eighteenth green. The kidney shaped green was the one of the most nuanced and interesting greens on the course. Its removal was also a removal of a part of the course's and Club's history. It was a green where dramatic putts and iron shots had determined the outcome of matches for Julius Boros, Arnold Palmer, and Jack Benson. It was also the green where Bobby Greenwood, Jamie Gonzales, and John Cook made dramatic birdies on the final hole to win the Sunne-

Jack Nicklaus putts on the original eighteenth green in 1956.

hanna Amateur. The new green was located to the left of the original green. The straight fairway was jogged to the left as well.

A Return to Its Roots

Ron Forse

In 1994, Sunnehanna's Grounds Committee decided to elicit the advice of Ron Forse of Forse Design and Frontier Construction to review the course and establish a long range plan. Among the principle goals was to return Sunnehanna back to one of the top ten courses in the state and to revive original Tillinghast features. An established plan could also provide continuity for succeeding Grounds Chairman. More importantly, it was hoped that it would end the cycle of each Chairman putting his personal "imprimatur" on the course.

Regrettably, other club projects delayed the immediate execution of this plan. If the plan was initiated when proposed, Sunnehanna would have been on the cutting edge of what became a national renaissance of classic golf courses. The restoration of the course initially began in 1994 as selected bunkers were restored. Dramatic tree removal also took place.

In 2002, the Grounds Committee enacted an ambitious list of projects for the course. Four years earlier, a modest program to return the greens to there original size began. A more aggressive plan was adopted and lost features began to re-emerge.

The most significant and important project was re-instatement of the cross-bunker on fifteen in 2003. Forse's plan stated, "When done this could be the best hole on the course." This opinion was based on the large bunker that originally bisected the fairway. Previously ignored, Forse understood the architectural significance of the double-dogleg par five and the bunker.

Another important job undertaken was the removal of trees. The success of tree removal programs, most notably at Oakmont, had evoked admiration throughout golf. Like Oakmont, Sunnehanna was originally an inland links. A controversial and emotional issue at any club, the decision to remove trees was long overdue.

The USGA, in its annual evaluation of the course, had for years attributed many problems to Mother Nature's sentinels. Turf and drainage troubles at Sunnehanna could be directly attributed to the over-planting of trees in the 1950's. The lack of a comprehensive tree maintenance plan exacerbated the problem. The first steps of returning the great views afforded golfers and members alike have just begun.

The Golf Course

Retrospective

In Sunnehanna's eighty years of existence, golf's finest architects imparted their knowledge and expertise over it's rolling hills. Reminders of their influence remain, some subtle, some obvious. It began in 1921 with A.W. Tillinghast's original design. Emil Loeffler gave sustenance to the starved ground and guidance to a novice Grounds Committee. Having survived the Depression, William Flynn was hired and made significant and lasting contributions to the course. William Gordon provided advice and a par-four that accelerated the heart rates of the best amateur golfers in the world. Keeping the talents of all four in mind, Ron Forse worked to revive the best of their contributions.

Eighty years later, the routing of the golf course has remained essentially the same, a rarity in golf. It is a testament to Tillinghast's spectacular original plan. Sunnehanna's golf course has a pedigree that few clubs in the game can match. It is a reason for pride and awe for Sunnehanna Country Club's members and those who play it.

May 2004

The works of a great architect and the beauty of Sunnehanna

"It was a classic course—nothing flashy, no wild layouts, or crazy obstructions. It's a thinking player's course. You can't go to sleep on it."

Ben Crenshaw

The fourth hole, 1955

View from behind the second hole

Looking back toward the third hole

Behind the twelfth green

The opening view

The sixteenth

A Tillinghast Legacy

$\mathcal{A}$.W. Tillinghast left Johnstown and Sunnehanna Country Club with an outstanding golf course that has tested the skills of the golfers for over eighty years. He incorporated many of his most important design ideas, some subtle others more obvious on a canvas of barren land.

A believer in aesthetics, Tillinghast layered holes one behind another when possible using the green and surrounding bunkers of one hole as a backdrop for another.

View from the first tee, 1953

On Sunnehanna's first hole, Tillinghast used the eighth hole and its numerous bunkers as a back drop for the first green. He incorporated the same principle on the third hole, with the thirteenth hole behind it; and on seventeen, with the eleventh green and its bunkers as a backdrop. This simple artistic idea was eradicated over time by the elimination of bunkers and the planting of trees

Another important, but subtle concept was the idea of using triangles to layout the course. This idea eliminated boring parallel holes and straight lines. A quick look at an aerial photo of Sunnehanna of Tillinghast's design map and this principle will be evident throughout the course.

Tillinghast also created uncertainty on several of Sunnehanna's toughest holes. Taking full advantage of Sunnehanna's terrain, Tillinghast incorporated a principle he simply called deception. Second shots were played into greens without backdrops making it difficult to discern the width or depth of the greens. Approach shots into the second, sixth, ninth holes and eighteenth holes were made more difficult as golfers looked into a vacant sky. Deception also added to another nemesis for golfers: uncertainty.

A Tillinghast Legacy

Sunnehanna's Par Threes

Tillinghast's stated, "No course is any greater than its one shot holes. These should be standouts, altogether imposing and inspiring." Sunnehanna's par three's are the strength of the course. He believed in a distribution of distances of 125 yards, 160, 175 and 195. Sunnehanna was almost spot on when it was originally laid out. (Note: today fourteen is a par three but was originally a par four). The diversity of distances combined with elevation changes required golfers to use different clubs, different ball flights and some imagination.

Two par threes, the short tenth and the long seventh, incorporate two concepts frequently used by the architect.

Sunnehanna's Tiny Tim, the tenth.

Tiny Tim's

Tillinghast rarely utilized frontal bunkers in his designs, approach shots into Sunnehanna's par fours and pars fives are perfect examples. The exception were short par threes, like Sunnehanna's tenth hole. Tillinghast affectionately called holes of 150 yards or less the "Tiny Tims" of golf.

"The Tiny Tim is the one situation which causes me to depart from two convictions which have influenced me so long, and these concern the rear trap and the frontal hazard, which represents the obligatory carry", he wrote.

"Tillinghast did not believe a boldly played shot that is long on a par three should be penalized. A poorly played shot on a short par three should. As for the frontal, obligatory trap, this type of hole certainly causes me to draw away from my objection to it. Here the range of carry is fixed and most any class of player, even the most humble, should be able to carry trouble immediately in front of a 125 yard green."

When it came to the Tiny Tim green, Tillinghast remained steadfast in his approach. He wanted the surface to be modest in difficulty and slope, "The floor of the green should be entirely free of undulations, for luck figures so prominently when pitched balls strike on undulating surfaces. This does not mean that such a green must be monotonously plain-far from it. But the effects of impressive contouring are to be introduced from the outside edges with vigorous flarings to meet the pits."

A Tillinghast Legacy

Tillinghast utilized smaller greens for shorter shots and knew a green with severe undulations would limit pin placements.

The Long One-Shotter

The seventh hole is the antithesis of the tenth hole. An imposing downhill par three of 227-yards, Tillinghast utilized a totally different approach to the green and

The seventh, 1955. Smoke in the distance comes from the steel mills in the valley below.

surrounding hazards. Tillinghast wrote, "the design of any green that is to take a long wood from the tee is considered, it must of necessity be an open and spread out affair, gradually losing distinctive character as the length of the shot increases." This principle accounts for the essentially flat green on the seventh hole.

Tillinghast believed in providing players spectacular views to distract them from the challenge ahead. "We have now arrived at the conclusion that a one-shot hole, played from a stirring height, which should greet the eye with inspiration of lovely scenic beauty or panoramic grandeur and to a green a trifle sort of 200 yards." The seventh hole perfectly meets this description.

Tillinghast's original design for the long seventh.

He wanted players of all abilities to enjoy the long par three: "Even a duffer gets great kick as his shot goes zooming forth in an amazingly cheering way." While he wanted the "duffer" to enjoy the illusion of a long shot, he also didn't want to reward poor shots that barely got airborne: "The player should look down on a hazard sufficiently imposing as to make it necessary to regard the shot from the tee with some respect." This large hazard was in the original plan but was not included in the final design.

Using Nature and a Diversity of Shots

Every par three at Sunnehanna requires differently shaped shots played to greens with a variety of slopes. The fifth and sixteenth holes, while the same distance, require substantially different shots. The slopes of the greens

A Tillinghast Legacy

are the opposite of the other.

Tillinghast also shrewdly utilized the prevailing winds to add to the difficulty of each par three. The tenth, the shortest hole, plays into the wind, the seventh—the longest plays down wind. Both five and sixteen play into a left-to-right crosswind, the most difficult wind for right handed players. On five, Tillinghast took advantage of the prevailing wind and the left to right slope of the land to make a formidable par three. The green slopes severely from left to right. Originally players approach shots were encouraged to be played left toward four deep bunkers. On the right side he added a fifty yard long bunker to catch a sliced shot made worse by the wind. The addition of the ponds and a more elevated tee has somewhat changed the hole but the fifth hole remains a dynamic and difficult par three.

The Three-Shotter: Sunnehanna's Fifteenth

Tillinghast loathed the non-descript long par five, "Certainly there is no satisfaction in blazing away on such a hole, so utterly lacking in features which require finesse and accurate play. There must be something along the line which makes one think, something to invite brave endeavor and a suitable reward for the accomplishment." He believed that the ideal par five was a combination of a good par four and a short par three.

Tillinghast's sketch of his three shotter. Sunnehanna's fifteenth closely follows this concept.

The most important architectural concept that Tillinghast used at Sunnehanna was the double-dog-leg par five. Within the double-dog-leg he added the cross bunker, or as he called it a great hazard, "that big break across the fairway is to present a fair but fine carry for any second shot which is to open the green to the third, and at the same time stop anything which has not been well played from getting to the green at all. He repeatedly utilized the cross-bunker on many of his best known courses: Baltusrol's seventeenth, Bethpage Black's fourth, and Quaker Ridge's fourteenth to name just a few.

Players had to avoid bunkers with every shot on fifteen. The tee shot had to miss the boomerang bunker, which was also a greenside bunker on thirteen. The second shot had to carry the large cross bunker. A fairway bunker on thirteen was positioned to influence two holes. Another cross-bunker, it could capture poor tee shots on thirteen and shots sent left to evade the large hazard on fifteen. The fairway on fifteen, when finally moved, will be further right than

Sunnehanna's fifteenth

it s current location. Shots will be played to an open green which slopes away from the player. Presently, shots are played from the left and into the slope of the green. The ball initially spins left slowing the ball rather than a first bounce that would be forward if played from the right. Originally, a shot from a wrong angle would retreat to the back of the green.

When the fairway is moved it will also give players greater flexibility when contemplating whether to play short of the bunker or carry it. Shots played over the right side of the bunker are shorter than those to the left. It also leaves a longer approach shot into the green, which was surrounded by five deep bunkers.

The Putting Green

"The character of the putting greens and their approaches mark the quality of a course to a far extent than anything else," Tillinghast wrote. "No matter how excellent may be the distances: how cunningly placed the hazards, or how carefully considered has been the distribution of shots, if the greens themselves do not stand forth impressively the course itself can never be notable."

Tillinghast departed from some of his principles when he built Sunnehanna's greens. While detesting sloppy iron play, which he felt large greens rewarded, Tillinghast made concessions at Sunnehanna. He built larger putting surfaces in keeping with a links course. He understood that the treeless hillside course could be significantly influenced by nature. Players needed larger surfaces to compensate for potentially difficult winds. While the greens were larger, Tillinghast penalized errant shots with treacherous bunkers that made a satisfactory recovery difficult.

A feature Tillinghast did use throughout his courses was low spots located on the backs of greens. Intended to penalize approach shots from the wrong angle or with no spin, these low spots were designed to throw the ball into a surrounding bunker. This will return when the original green sizes are restored. The raised backs of the greens will also return pitch shots and bunker shots into downhill affairs as originally intended. When Sunnehanna's greens are firm and fast, players witness Tillinghast's original

View from behind the third green, fall 2003.

intent as approach shots played from a wrong position will typically leave the putting surface.

Over time, many interesting features on Sunnehanna's greens vanished, lost as a result of financial considerations during the Depression and gas rationing during World War II. Benign indifference and neglect to theses slopes resulted in greens shaped like saucers. The shrunken greens took greenside bunkers out of play as rough prevented balls from reaching the intended resting place: cavernous bunkers. A program to return the greens to their original sizes has resulted in the re-emergence of lost slopes.

Tillinghast's Legacy in Johnstown

A.W. Tillinghast designed and built Sunnehanna during the prime of his career. The rebirth of his legacy and a greater awareness of his influence on American golf have led to a greater appreciation of his knowledge and brilliance. A.W. Tillinghast gave Sunnehanna Country Club a visual masterpiece. A walk over it's rolling hills continues to challenge players of all abilities. A program is underway to bring back many of the features that exist in his original plan. Today, golfers face many of the same challenges that were introduced over eighty years ago by one of the geniuses of American golf architecture.

A summer's day in 1965

The Caddies of Brownstown

Their days started with a half-hour walk from Brownstown through the hilly slopes of Stackhouse Park to Sunnehanna. Golf was a cornerstone of community activity, as youngsters caddied and then played golf over two courses made by residents known as The Flat and The Level. The Flat offered four holes ranging from 150 to 300 yards; The Level had three holes. The two courses provided endless hours of golf for kids and were the breeding grounds for an impressive list of fine players.

What course you played depended on what side of town you lived on. A natural rivalry took place between the two courses: "We had the better players on our side of the hill. The Gallaghers, Witprachtigers, Zimmers, Leshinskys and Schnecks all were good players," stated Bob Hahn, who has been head professional for thirty-five years at Immergrun, Charles Schwab's one-time private course now operated by St. Francis University in Loretto.

Caddying at Sunnehanna was a right of passage for the boroughs youngsters, "It was something that was expected of you. You knew you got to a certain age, you'd caddy. That was a given," said Tom Helsel, former president of the Brownstown Golf Association. It was also a close knit fraternity: of the 250 caddies at Sunnehanna, 220 or so came from Brownstown. "The first thing you were asked was, Hey kid where are you from, if you said Brownstown you were in," recalled Bob Hahn.

The $1.25 earned for eighteen holes or $.75 for nine holes helped families make ends meet during difficult times." The annual caddy tournament champion received an extra benefit "You got to shag balls when the pro gave lessons. You got paid $.50 a lesson and he gave about eight lessons a day, I felt like the richest guy in town," said Frank Kiraly who won the caddy tournament numerous times.

Twenty-two of Brownstown caddies became head professionals at various clubs, mostly in Western Pennsylvania, but some found success beyond. Jim Gallagher left Brownstown finding employment in Marion, Indiana as an assistant professional and later became Head Professional. His son, Jim, and daughter, Jackie, also became professionals winning tournaments on the PGA and LPGA tours.

The golf course and caddy yard at Sunnehanna gave them an education for a better future. Frank Kiraly and Steve Gaydos were the two best players and were role models for future generations. The wiry Gaydos, who was Head Professional at North Fork and Somerset Country Club, used his prodigious length to

Frank Kiraly

surpass the PGA Tour's best. In the national long drive contest at Oakland Hills, Gaydos easily defeated Mike Souchak and Sam Snead to win the title.

The finest player to ever come from the Johnstown area was Frank Kiraly. Kiraly served as Head Professional at five area courses and played in four U.S. Opens and five PGA Championships. He attributes his success in golf to his days at Sunnehanna, " When I was 14, they let us caddies play on

Toney Penna, Jimmy Demaret, Brownstown's Steve Gaydos and Sunnehanna Professional Carl Beljan.

Mondays. The members lent us their clubs. They taught us to be gentlemen. It was the best upbringing. They would spend time teaching us to be caddies. They even had a written exam." At seventeen, Kiraly ran the golf operations at Sunnehanna as fighting-aged men left for military service. In 1976, he was named a PGA Master Professional and inducted into the Tri-State PGA Hall of Fame in 1989.

Brownstown golf has disappeared with time. The Flat is now covered with trees and shrubs, The Level is a playground and park, but the legacy they left are the lives altered by the pleasure and opportunity they once gave others. Bob Hahn said it best, "Everything I have in life is because of caddying at Sunnehanna and golf."

Eddie Vetock: A Remarkable Man

Another caddie who came from Brownstown didn't play on The Flat or The Level or become a golf professional but was the greatest success story of all the caddies. Eddie Vetock came to Sunnehanna at the same age as most, but was met with derision by some. Eddie was different; he had Down's Syndrome. The arrival of John Goettlicher as Head Professional changed his life and gave him the opportunity to grow as a person. He didn't just grow, he thrived, and became an integral part of the everyday rhythm of Sunnehanna. His sense of humor and devotion to friends was legendary. Everyone has an Eddie story that brings smiles or chuckles but not at his expense. The most legend-

ary story was upon returning from Germany, where he visited his brother, caddies asked if he caddied for Hitler. Eddied replied, "No he took a cart." His nicknames for various professional golfers brought laughter to all golfers, Johnny Miller was John Motor, Jack Nicklaus was Jack Nixon, Lee Trevino was Lee the Beaver; the list was endless.

Eddie first caddied in the Sunnehanna Amateur for Ed Updegraff. Later, Sunnehanna members Bill Crooks and Phil Saylor utilized his talents during the tournament. Eddie's excitement knew no bounds, continually informing everyone that Bill or Phil was going to win the tournament. During the tournament, Eddie did create a problem for Phil Saylor. Saylor's tee shot went astray on the ninth hole and a search ensued–Eddie, ever helpful, located the ball and picked it up exclaiming, "Here Phil, here's your ball." A violation of the rules, Phil asked Eddie why he picked the ball up. His quick response, "Jay Sigel (Saylor's playing partner) told me to."

Eddie's birthday was a big occasion and he made sure everyone knew about his special day. By days end, Eddie had new hats and shirts, compliments of various members. Almost every year Martin Goldhaber bought him a new suit.

In 1979, he was featured in *The Tribune Democrat* Weekender section. Titled Eddie Vetock: A Success Story chronicled his extraor-

Ed Vetock and Bill Crooks

dinary life. Sunnehanna was an emptier place when Eddie retired from caddying in 1984. Twenty years after he left, Eddie Vetock's name brings a universal response to those who knew him a smile. His intelligence, sense of humor, and amazing spirit are forever imbedded in our memories.

Thank you, Eddie.

The **S***unnehanna* **I***nvitational*

1936 - 1951

The Beginning of Championship Golf at Sunnehanna Country Club

Sunnehanna Invitational
1936-1951

*I*n 1936, Sunnehanna Country Club, capitalizing on strong member and growing regional interest in tournament golf, introduced the Sunnehanna Invitational, inviting the best players from Johnstown and throughout central and western Pennsylvania. Aware of the financial success of similar events at other country clubs, the club's Board was attracted to the potential additional revenue during the Depression.

The first tournament was an immediate success and became an annual event except for the war years. The post war period attracted the best players from the east coast, among them Arnold Palmer, Art Wall, and Julius Boros.

A major part of the tournament was the popular Calcutta, where members bid on players they felt might win the championship flight. Initially, the Calcutta was an asset helping generate keen member interest. Eventually, the gambling became a problem and the Club's Board of Governors terminated the tournament after 1951.

A Strong Start

The inaugural Sunnehanna Invitational, held in August 1936, was the first time Sunnehanna Country Club welcomed golfers from throughout western Pennsylvania to compete on its hilltop course. The headlines of the *Johnstown Daily Tribune* read "Big Invitation Golf Tourney Planned" as club president, Wilson Slick, appointed a governing tournament committee that included himself, C.R. Ellicot, W.A. Reiber, M.J. McCleary, Manual Mendelson, and John Cook.

Golfers throughout the area lacked opportunities to play competitive golf and were excited by the prospect of playing Sunnehanna's exclusive and highly acclaimed course. Designed by one of golf's preeminent architects, Albert Warren Tillinghast, players throughout the area heard of, but rarely had played the course. The overwhelmingly positive responses from golfers made Slick believe the tournament was sure to become an annual event on Sunnehanna's calendar.

The tournament's format mirrored other country club Invitational's throughout the nation. Played over three days, the event started with an eighteen-hole stroke play qualifying round on the first day. Players were then paired based on their qualifying score into sixteen-player match play brackets.

Various social events were held during the tournament. None was more important than Thursday night's Calcutta. The Calcutta auction was opened only to members and was held after the first day's qualifying round. The players who qualified for the championship flight were placed in an auction, members then bid on each player, starting with an opening bid of $200. If the player won, the 'owner' took home half the pot, while the remaining funds were divided among the 'owners' of the runner-up and semi-finalists. The money in the Calcutta added significant interest to the matches.

Sunnehanna Invitational

Local Players Dominate

In 1936, Sunnehanna's first Invitational boasted a field of 200 participants. After three days of play, two Sunnehanna members reached the finals: Dr. Joseph McHugh defeated Dr. George Wheeling to win the inaugural event.

The following year eight Sunnehanna members qualified for the championship flight and Joseph McHugh successfully defended his title, defeating fellow member, Cecil C. McClain.

Wheeling reached the finals again in 1938 and faced Earl Hewitt from Indiana for the title. Hewitt, the Invitational medalist in 1937, out-played the Windber physician, winning the tournament 4&3.

The 1939 tourney was the first time that the Invitational finals matched two players without local ties. William "Skinny" Lewis, a 19-year old from Reading, Pennsylvania defeated L. B. Peterson from Steubenville, Ohio, 5&4. Lewis shared the course record at his home club, Berkshire Country Club, with the 1939 U.S. Open Champion, Byron Nelson.

The next year Sunnehanna members, McClain and Wheeling returned to the finals. In spite of torrential rains that delayed the championship match, over 500 spectators followed the finalists. The two-time Invitational runner-up, Wheeling defeated defending champion, Lewis, as well as former champions Hewitt and McHugh to play for the title. McClain, two-down after 13 holes, won four straight holes to capture the title.

State Champions Compete

Until 1940, the Invitational failed to attract a state amateur champion to the tournament. In 1941, there were two: Steve Kovach, the reigning Pennsylvania State Amateur and West Penn Open Champion from Brackenridge, and Johnny Markel, also from Berkshire Country Club and the Pennsylvania Scholastic Champion.

The Tribune provided broad coverage to the 1941 tournament. Here it covers Steve Kovach's victory in great detail, including the large gallery following the players.

Small in stature, Kovach's game possessed power and length, developed from his day job as a steelworker in Homestead. Kovach defeated Jack Phelan of Ridgeway 6&5, as the mill hands presence attracted the largest crowds in the Invitational's history. Later that summer, Kovach reached the quarter-finals of the U.S. Amateur and successfully defended his Pennsylvania State Amateur the next year.

Sunnehanna Invitational

Without competition from television coverage, large crowds walked Sunnehanna's fairways to watch top flight amateur golf in 1941.

In 1946, Kovach turned professional after returning home from military service and captured the Pennsylvania State Open title. He won the title again in 1947. Among the competitors he defeated was the recently crowned U.S. Open Champion, Lew Worsham.

Rebounding From War

The war ended competitive golf nationally, as Sunnehanna followed the USGA's lead and suspended the Invitational tournament. From 1942 through 1945, the nation struggled to meet basic needs; frivolous diversions, like tournament golf, gave way to more practical concerns.

By 1946, the nation was returning to its pre-war routines, and with this came the return of competitive golf. The Invitational's growing reputation prior to the war, coupled with the Eastern Amateur's demise, drew 141 players from throughout the East Coast to Johnstown. In response to this growth, the tournament committee expanded the championship bracket from 16 to 32 contestants and the championship match lengthened to 36 holes.

In the Invitational's brief history, 1946 was the strongest field to-date as five tournament players qualified later that year for the U.S. Amateur at Baltusrol. It was also the most financially successful Invitational, as the Club turned a profit of $1900, and the Calcutta pool reached a record high of $8705.

Art Wall was the medalist in the 1946 Invitational. He returned to Sunnehanna in 1965 to give an exhibition. Wall had a successful career on the PGA tour winning 14 times, highlighted by remarkable victory in the 1959 Masters. He birdied five of the final six holes to defeat Cary Middlecoff by a single stroke.

Among the early favorites in 1946 was Air Force veteran and Duke University golfer Art Wall of Honesdale, Pennsylvania. Wall established a new qualifying record, firing a scintillating round of 67 to capture medalist honors.

In his first-round match, Wall was six-down after six holes to Jack Brand of Oakmont. After twelve holes, he made an incredible comeback to square the match, and dispose of his opponent two-up. Wall's putter failed him in his second match losing to former Sunnehanna member, Don O'Conner, two- down.

The finals matched Bill Haverstick, the 1938 Pennsylvania State Amateur Champion and 1939 National Intercollegiate Championship runner-up while at Swathmore College, against two-time Invitational champion, Joseph McHugh. Huge galleries witnessed a 10 and 9 whipping, as Haverstick dominated play in the championship final.

Haverstick Defeats Dr. McHugh by Wide Margin For Sunnehanna Invitational Golf Championship

Big Golf Gallery Sees Climax of Sunnehanna Championship Match

Bill Haverstick, right, and runner-up Dr. Joseph McHugh shake hands after the 1946 finals. Huge galleries saw Haverstick dominate play winning 10 and 9.

Over the next four years, Wall and Haverstick were the Keystone State's premier players winning the Pennsylvania State Amateur, in alternate years, from 1947 through 1951.

In 1947, Haverstick captured medalist honors, but was upset in the first round. The finals pit Reading sensation Buddy Lutz against Johnstown native, Charles Kunkle. Kunkle defeated Lutz's good friend and four-ball partner Billy Eben in the semi-finals to reach the championship match.

Nicknamed the 'Reading Rocket', Lutz sent a strong message with his first swing as his drive traveled 380 yards from the elevated first tee. Lutz never trailed in the match, recording nine birdies over 30 holes and closed out the match with three consecutive birdies, disposing of Kunkle 10&8.

Lutz credited a large flanged wedge given to him by his hometown professional Henry Poe for some of his success. "It worked great at Sunnehanna that year. The course was burned out and hardpan, and I drove Charlie Kunkle crazy with it," he recalled.

Bob Drum, a legendary writer for the *Pittsburgh Post-Gazette* who frequently covered the Sunnehanna Invitational from darkened confines of the men's basement grill, provided a colorful description of Lutz's play that day: "Buddy Lutz takes after his dad. They both bury people. Buddy does it to his opponents on the golf course while Papa Lutz runs an undertaking business in Reading."

Sunnehanna Invitational

The Future Of Golf

While Buddy Lutz won the title, the 1947 Invitational marked the debut of a teenage standout named Arnold Palmer. In 1946, Palmer won the Pennsylvania Scholastic Champion and qualified for the Hearst National Junior Open, one of junior golf's most prestigious tournaments. Palmer reached the finals in his first exposure to national competition and displayed the skills and personality that later became world famous.

Palmer was enjoying another successful summer before his arrival at Sunnehanna in 1947. He defended his Pennsylvania Scholastic title, won the West Penn Junior title and reached the semi-finals of the PA State Amateur before losing to Art Wall. Exhausted by his non-stop tournament schedule, Palmer shot 83 at Sunnehanna, missing the qualifying score of 79 needed to reach the championship flight. Palmer quickly recovered from his performance in Johnstown, winning the West Penn Amateur defeating Knox Young, a two-time champion of both the Pennsylvania and West Penn Amateur. With that victory, Palmer became only the third player to win both the West Penn Junior and Amateur titles in the same year, joining Barrett Melvin and Fred Brand.

In July of 1948, Palmer returned to Sunnehanna determined to erase the memory of his previous years' performance. Already that month, he won his second West Penn Junior title. A week before competing in the Invitational, he made the cut in his first PGA event: the Dapper Dan Invitational Open at Alcoma Country Club in Pittsburgh.

Palmer easily qualified for match play, shooting two-under par 70, to

Arnold Palmer's failure to qualify was big news in Latrobe. Palmer came to Sunnehanna for the first time in 1947, having won several titles.

A young Arnold Palmer (center) checks the 1948 scoreboard with Charles Kunkle (left) and Bud Griffith (right). Palmer won the 1948 Invitational. Kunkle would win the Invitational in 1950.

Sunnehanna Invitational

finish one stroke behind medalist Spencer Overton, the 1947 Maryland Open Champion. Palmer reached the finals by defeating defending champion Buddy Lutz 3&2, and Bill Vaile of North Fork 5&4.

In the finals, Palmer struggled early trailing three-down after seven holes to Jacob 'Babe' Matlack an unheralded player from Blairmont Country Club. *Post-Gazette* writer Bob Drum was not impressed by Palmer's opponent's ball striking; "Matlack doesn't play the shots most of the top-notch amateurs in the district can. He is addicted to the blooper, grounder, and head lift until he gets to the green. Then it is Matlack's turn to shine."

Matlack's uncanny short game wore on the Latrobe native as time-and – time again he saved par from the most unlikely places. After the morning eighteen, the underdog Matlack stood one-up after pitching in three times from off the green.

Matlack pushed the match to the final hole, but found a greenside bunker with his approach shot. Palmer, safely on the green in two, watched as his opponent took two shots to extricate himself from the sand. Two putts later, Palmer closed out his opponent, winning the championship, two-up.

The Locker Room Legend

Arnold Palmer, now a student at Wake Forest, didn't return to defend his title in 1949 instead he competed in the National Intercollegiate Collegiate championships. While Palmer was missed, the 1949 Sunnehanna Invitational had its best field ever with 150 entrants from nine states. Three over par 75 was needed to qualify for the Championship Flight, the lowest cut in the tournament's history. Among the many top players in the field was the best amateur golfer on the East Coast, Julius Boros from Hartford, Connecticut.

The medalist and semi-finalist in the 1948 U.S. Amateur, Boros had lead the 1948 North-South Open, a notable tournament on the PGA tour, for 63-holes, only to falter down the stretch to finish tied for second. Boros carded an eagle and five birdies to shoot six-under par 66 and establish a new tournament record qualifying score. Jack Benson of South Hills and Jack Mahaffey of Oakmont, were his closest competitors with 69s. Boros continued his hot play the next day in his morning match by playing thirteen holes in five-under par to defeat Greensburg's Tommy Smith 6&5.

In Boros' second match, local player Danny Moore provided stiffer resistance for the tournament medalist. After Boros birdied thirteen and fifteen to take a one-up lead, Moore squared the match on seventeen with a birdie. Then on eighteen, Boros' approach shot from 100 yards finished in a bunker guarding the green. The tournament favorite failed to save par and Moore won the hole, and the match, with a routine par. Moore's victory was the greatest upset in the Invitational's history.

Before packing his bags and returning home, Boros reflected on his loss to reporters in the locker room. "Trying to win one of these amateur tourna-

Newspaper article details Arnold Palmer's 1948 win.

ments is tougher than winning on the tour," he explained. "You visit various places and meet players you never heard of and they all can play. Any kind of let-up and you're out of the tournament in match play."

Someone asked Boros why not turn professional, and play only 72 holes of stroke play. Boros replied, "That's just what I've been thinking about." A few months later, Julius Boros joined the PGA Tour.

In 1949, Julius Boros established a new qualifying record of 6 under par 66. Boros won two U.S. Open titles in 1952 and 1963 plus the P.G.A. title in 1968. His professional career included 18 PGA tour titles and he was leading money winner in 1952 and 1963.

Lutz's Improbable Comeback

The 1949 Invitational finals saw the return of 1947 Champion Buddy Lutz. Also making a return to amateur golf after a three-year hiatus was Jack Benson, five-time winner of the West Penn Amateur.

Benson played spectacular golf to reach the finals, cruising around the Sunnehanna layout in 12-under par over his three previous matches.

In the finals, Benson held a solid three-up lead over Lutz through the first 30 holes, until severe thunderstorms suspended play. When play resumed, Benson stretched his lead to a seemingly insurmountable four-up lead with five holes to play. Lutz rallied with birdies on fourteen and fifteen. On sixteen, Lutz narrowly missed a hole-in-one on the par-three, the ball finishing one foot from the cup.

On seventeen, Lutz nailed a 275-yard drive on the course's toughest hole, and found the green with a seven iron. Two putts later, Buddy Lutz and Jack Benson were all square. At the 377-yard eighteenth hole, a shell-shocked Benson hit the better drive. Lutz played first, his shot landing on the green finishing some 20 feet from the pin. Benson's approach shot came up short and his subsequent chip shot ended eight-feet short of the cup. Lightning struck twice as Lutz relied on his Spalding Cash-In putter to complete the improbable comeback, bury-

Lutz Presented Well-Earned Trophy

James Ashcom, Sunnehanna Country Club President presents Buddy Lutz with the Championship Trophy as runner-up Jack Benson looks on. Lutz won the last five holes to win one up. It was the second Invitational title for the 21 year old, having previously won in 1947.

ing his birdie putt to capture his second Invitational title, one-up.

The *Pittsburgh Post* writer Phil Gundlefinger called the final match and Lutz's remarkable comeback, "Perhaps the most sensational finish in Pennsylvania golf history, either amateur or professional." It was the finest moment in Lutz's amateur career.

"I can still hear the crowd today, I hit the putt too hard, the ball jumped five or six inches in the air then went in the hole," Buddy Lutz recalled in an interview. As for Jack Benson's reaction after the match he told Lutz, "I'll give Ben Hogan that lead and he won't beat me."

Lutz, who played in five U.S. Amateurs and three U.S. Opens, fondly remembers Johnstown, and the Sunnehanna Invitational:

My best experiences in golf were at Sunnehanna. I traveled with my good friend Billy Eben and stayed every year, but the first, with Dr. George Wheeling...we had a great time. You weren't treated better anywhere. The Sunnehanna Invitational was the best tournament by far.

The USGA Speaks

While the Invitational was coming off its greatest tournament ever, black clouds were gathering over amateur golf. Two weeks after completion of the 1949 Invitational, the United States Golf Association (USGA) warned that Calcuttas, or auction pools, would eventually damage golf's integrity.

Sunnehanna Invitational

In a full-page statement, the USGA expressed great concern that professional gambling could take over the sport. James Walker, Chairman of the USGA Amateur Status and Conduct Committee asserted, "Organized auction pools would almost certainly run into large figures and lead to commercializing the game to a high degree, and might well be the means for professional gamblers to take over and influence players, just as they have done in other sports."

While not citing specific tournaments or players, the USGA alluded to possibly cracking down on amateur players who bet heavily on their own skills, as well as tournaments they considered dubious amateur competitions. With golf's ruling body now watching tournaments like the Sunnehanna Invitational, changes were eminent.

Coincidently, the Invitational's Calcutta in 1949 was compromised by members of Johnstown's gambling fraternity. The pool exceeded $30,000, with a single $20,000 bid wagered on Buddy Lutz. The Calcutta was now a liability, not an asset.

Sunnehanna's Board of Governors unanimously passed a resolution that ended the Calcutta at their meeting on January 18, 1950.

The results of the Board's action were immediate as the quality of the field slipped and membership interest waned without the Calcutta. In spite of these obstacles, the tournament pushed forward, providing two additional years of memorable moments and outstanding golf.

The Final Years

In 1950, Charles Kunkle returned to the finals and won the Championship, defeating Stewart Brown of Yale University 6 and 5. Kunkle was denied the opportunity to avenge his loss in 1947 to Buddy Lutz who was recovering from an appendectomy.

A field of just over 100 players vied for the final Sunnehanna Invitational title in 1951. Bill Haverstick captured medalist honors just ahead of 1949 Invitational finalist Jack Benson.

An early match attracted considerable attention and added one final legendary story to the Invitational's history. Two-time champion, Buddy Lutz was pitted against 16-year old Johnny Felus, a caddie from Cresson Country Club. Felu stood five feet tall, weighed 108 pounds, and walked the course in tennis shoes and blue jeans.

Despite his first-round junior tournament loss at the Johnstown Municipal golf course, Felus played with the confidence of a seasoned veteran. One-up after five holes, Felus neatly reached the green in two [on the par-five sixth hole with a two-iron from a fairway bunker. Lutz complemented Felus on the fine shot, to which he replied, "Now I'm going to sink the putt," which he did for an eagle-three.

Lutz trailed his youthful pest after twelve holes, two-down. Then in an amazing coincidence, a heavy rain suspended play on the thirteenth hole, just

Sunnehanna Invitational

Jack Benson strokes the winning putt on the 39th hole to defeat Charles Kunkle in the 1951 Sunnehanna Invitational.

as it had two years earlier. When play resumed, Lutz responded like before, winning the next five holes to defeat Felus 3&1. Inspired by Felus' spirited play, tournament players chipped in and presented him with a pair of golf shoes and a set of woods.

In the semi-finals, Kunkle, recovering from a broken thumb which forced him to use a baseball grip, defeated Lutz 2 and 1. Kunkle then met Jack Benson in the finals.

After 35 holes of play, Kunkle held a one-up lead. On eighteen, Kunkle missed a three-foot putt and Benson evened the match with a par. On the 39th hole, both players reached the green in regulation. Kunkle missed his twelve-footer for birdie, and Benson responded making his ten-foot birdie putt, claiming the twelfth and final Sunnehanna invitational title.

Benson reached the semi-finals of the U.S. Amateur later that summer. Three years later, in 1954, Benson added his sixth and final West Penn Amateur to his resume, a record that stands second only to William C. Fownes, an outstanding amateur golfer who later refined his father's original design of Oakmont.

Goodbye Invitational, Hello Amateur

After the 1951 Invitational, the Board of Governors ended the tournament. The decline in member interest, the diminished size and quality of the field, and the tournament losing money made terminating the Invitational an easy decision.

The Invitational evolved from a tournament comprised of essentially local players and grew into one of the finest events on the East Coast.

Arnold Palmer, Art Wall and Julius Boros, had very successful careers on the PGA tour. Invitational champions, Steve Kovach and Buddy Lutz, also turned professional and had modest success. Invitational participants such as Jack and Fred Brand, Charles Kunkle, Jack Mahaffey and Dick and Harton Semple became leaders within local, state, and national golf associations.

Fred Brand, was president of both the West Penn and Pennsylvania State Golf Associations and served on the USGA Executive Committee from 1958 to 1969. In 1966, Sunnehanna dedicated its seventh hole to Brand in recognition of his contributions to golf. He was a fine player winning numerous West Penn Golf Association titles and qualifying for many USGA championships.

Mahaffey also served as a member of the USGA's Executive Committee from 1975-1980, and was the General Chairman of the 1951 PGA Championship, 1969 U.S. Amateur and the 1973 U.S. Open.

Harton Semple, qualified for nine U.S. Amateurs, and was elected the USGA President in 1947 and 1975 after serving eight years on the Executive Committee. His daughter, Carol, became the pre-eminent woman's amateur golfer in the United States winning seven USGA championships.

These players represented the best of amateur golf in Pennsylvania and remained devoted to the game as players and volunteers.

The foundation laid by the Club, the Tournament Committee and the contestants led to competitive golf returning to Sunnehanna Country Club three years later.

The Sunnehanna Invitational brought both top amateur players and large crowds.

Witness to the Future of Golf
Arnold Palmer

Long before Tiger Woods, Arnold Palmer changed golf. Palmer burst on to the local and state golfing scene in 1946 winning the first of two Pennsylvania Interscholastic Athletic Association titles and the qualifier for the Hearst National Junior Open. The National Junior Open was Palmer's first exposure to national competition. Palmer reached the finals and faced Mac Hunter, the reigning Western Junior champion, in the championship match. Hunter defeated Palmer 6&5 and received the William Randolph Hearst Trophy, but Palmer impressed everyone who watched. Writer Tom Birks wrote afterward, "Palmer scintillated on the links today, showing power and precision in his tee shots and wonderful work on his short iron play". Throughout the event, the young Palmer won the hearts of spectators and players, as a large gallery followed the final match. Birks added, "Though losing the 16 year old Palmer, who is likewise a golf pro's son, nevertheless enhanced his links reputation. His play in the tourney stamped him as one of the outstanding junior golfers in the entire country. Furthermore, according to reporters who have been following the group of young stars throughout the four-day event, the general conduct of the Latrobean has definitely established him as one of the most popular players in the entire tournament."

Palmer's success was a source of tremendous community pride in Latrobe; his achievements were front page sports news. Palmer's growing reputation attracted large crowds. At Ligonier Country Club, Arnie played with his father, Deacon, in the Tri-State Pro-Am, six hundred fans came to watch father and son. Vincent Quatrini, sports editor for the local newspaper wrote about Palmer's influence: "The prevailing attitude was that golf was a rich man's game and that if you didn't play the game there was nothing to it from the onlooker's point of view." He added, "There was little interest in the game at Latrobe High School among the students. But talk to anyone of the students who were in school last season and they'll tell you exactly what Arnie did in every one of his matches. There were even some rabid followers of the golfing king that even played 'hook' from school to go to matches."

Before traveling to Johnstown in 1947, Palmer defended his Pennsylvania Scholastic title and won the West Penn Junior. In the Pennsylvania State Amateur, Palmer reached the semi-finals. The youngest player in the field, Palmer defeated Andy Szwedko, a former U.S. Public Links champion, in the third round before losing to eventual champion, Art Wall.

After faltering in the Sunnehanna Invitational, Palmer regrouped, winning the West Penn Amateur and becoming the third player to win both the West Penn Junior and Amateur titles in the same year. Palmer then qualified for the National Junior Open, but failed to match his previous year's performance losing in a first-round upset. Arnold Palmer was building the foundation for even greater success.

In July of 1948, Palmer won his second West Penn Junior title and the week before the Invitational, played in his first PGA event–The Dapper Dan Invitational and made the cut.

Palmer returned to Sunnehanna with his rabid followers who ventured over the hill to cheer on their hometown hero. In the semi-finals, Buddy Lutz recalled facing Palmer and his fanatical army, "I never was treated like that anywhere. His fans elbowed me and pushed me when I tried to get to my ball. They tried to intimidate me. I never had dealt with that before. I knew how Nicklaus felt at Oakmont in 1962."

Arnold Palmer returned to Johnstown in 1949, winning the North Fork Invitational.

While winning two titles in Friendly City, Palmer left behind an unpaid debt. Short on cash to buy sandwiches and a soft drink, Arnold borrowed $3.50 from Julius Eckel, a Sunnehanna member. He signed an I.O.U. for the loan, which he never repaid. Eckel carried the badly worn piece of paper in his wallet for the rest of his life showing it to anyone. He regaled about the best player in golf and his forgotten obligation.

Arnold Palmer's greatest accomplishments were still to come. His charisma, good looks and a game to match were just what the professional tour and television needed. He dominated professional golf in the early 60s capturing the U.S. Open (1960), British Open (1961, 1962) and The Masters (1958,1960, 1962,1964). His personality and modest background endeared him to the working man and attracted a new group of fans and participants to golf. Known as "Arnies Army", its roots could be traced to where it all began: Latrobe and Western Pennsylvania.

The Sunnehanna Amateur

1954-2003

The Sunnehanna Amateur

On March 25th, 1954, Club President Charles Kunkle presented for consideration to the Club's Board the concept of a national stroke play invitational tournament. Kunkle's idea of a 72-hole medal play tournament was revolutionary for amateur golf. A motion was made and properly carried and the Sunnehanna Amateur began.

The Sunnehanna Amateur differentiated itself from its predecessor, the Sunnehanna Invitational, in several ways. The most significant difference was the adoption of stroke or medal play. Another important goal was operating the tournament free of a Calcutta which had ended the successful Invitational.

Although used extensively by the PGA tour, major amateur tournaments remained wedded to tradition and resisted adopting stroke play. This was in spite of the belief that stroke play was considered superior to match play for determining a champion.

The tournament quickly evolved from a field of predominately regional players to attracting the best players from throughout the United States and beyond. By its third year, the Sunnehanna Amateur was being declared by some golf pundits as "the" national stroke play championship. The tournaments success changed the face of competitive golf. Some amateur tournaments changed their formats while other stroke play tournaments followed, such as the Northeast Amateur and Porter Cup.

Fifty years after it began, the Amateur continues to attract the nation's best golfers to Sunnehanna Country Club. From its nascent beginning, the Sunnehanna Amateur became, and remains, one of the majors of amateur golf. The Club's members and golf enthusiasts from Johnstown have watched players who became the best in the history of the game. Among the tournaments notable contestants were Jack Nicklaus, Tiger Woods, Lanny Wadkins, Curtis Strange, Fred Couples, Davis Love, and Phil Mickelson.

More than 120 PGA tour champions have played in the tournament. Thirty -six contestants have achieved professional golf's pinnacle of success: winning one of professional golf's four major championships, The Masters, the US Open, the British Open and the PGA Championship.

The tournament has produced notable champions such as Don Cherry, Dr. Ed Updegraff, Bill Hyndman, Bobby Greenwood, Ben Crenshaw, Jay Sigel, John Cook, Brad Faxon, Billy Andrade, Scott Verplank, and Allen Doyle.

The following pages are a testimony to their successes and participation in the Sunnehanna Amateur. It also acknowledges the tournament's important place in the history of American golf.

The Sunnehanna Amateur

DON CHERRY

*T*ournament golf was re-introduced at Sunnehanna Country Club in July of 1954 with a new format, medal play.

The inaugural Sunnehanna Amateur field had 20 entrants, including 11 golfers from Pennsylvania, six of whom were from Johnstown.

Sunnehanna Invitational champions Bill Haverstick (1946), the three-time Pennsylvania Amateur champion, and Jack Benson (1951) a six-time winner of the West Penn Amateur, returned to Sunnehanna. The most prominent players from beyond the boundaries of the Keystone State were Don Cherry from Wichita Falls, Texas via Las Vegas and Ed Tutwiler. Turwiler had just won his sixth West Virginia Amateur title.

Don Cherry

Don Cherry was the ideal contestant for the inaugural Sunnehanna Amateur. A member of the 1953 Walker Cup team and the Canadian Amateur champion in 1952, Cherry had the national reputation that the tournament committee wanted.

Cherry could entertain spectators on the course with his game and members off the course as well. A well known singer in the casinos of Las Vegas, Cherry had appeared on television programs such as the Colgate Comedy Hour and Bob Hope, to name a few. His vocal talents were invaluable to a committee in need of entertainment for the Club's members on Saturday evening.

On Friday July 16th at 2'o'clock Dick Burgoon from Carlisle, Pennsylvania struck the opening drive and tournament golf returned to Sunnehanna Country Club. At days end, Don Cherry led the tournament after a scintillating round of five-under par 65 which included six birdies. Three players Lynn Creason, former Pennsylvania Amateur champion, Don Hoenig and Ed Tutwiler were tied for second three strokes behind.

After four rounds of golf, Don Cherry defeated Don Hoenig, the former Connecticut Amateur champion from Putnam, Connecticut by four strokes.

Don Cherry left Sunnehanna with the winner's trophy and $500 in his pocket. Dr. George Wheeling, a civic leader and golf enthusiast, assumed the cost for Cherry singing on Saturday night.

The inaugural event was considered a great success by the players and members. The Sunnehanna Amateur would change the landscape of competitive amateur golf as medal play tournaments sprang up throughout the country within a few years.

Sunnehanna Amateur
HILLMAN ROBBINS

The second tournament was a testament to the appeal of medal play. The Sunnehanna Amateur consisted of 36 participants who had won 12 state amateur championships and two state opens the summer before. Only two players from Johnstown were invited to play.

Defending champion Don Cherry returned to defend his title. Cherry had recently participated in the Walker Cup at St. Andrews. Upon his return to the States, he appeared on several New York City radio stations to promote his hit song *Band of Gold* which had sold over a million copies. Because of the song's success, Cherry's standard singing fee increased to $750 for a night. Just as the year before, Dr. Wheeling generously assumed the cost.

Hillman Robbins accepts the winner's trophy. Robbins later won the US Amateur in 1957

The most prominent additions to the tournament were Dick Chapman and Hillman Robbins. Chapman was one of the few amateur golfers to win both the U.S Amateur (1946) and British Amateur (1944) championships. Robbins had won three titles in 1954: the Tennessee Amateur, Arkansas Open, and the National Intercollegiate Championship, the forerunner to the NCAA championship.

The tournament had a different leader after every round as Bill Haverstick, Dick Chapman, and Ed Tutwiler led after the first, second, and third rounds respectively. The outcome of the tournament was decided on the final two holes between Tutwiler, Robbins and Cherry.

On seventeen, Tutwiler's second shot found a greenside bunker and failed to save par. Robbins saved par from the same bunker to maintain a two stroke lead over Don Cherry. Cherry had chipped in for birdie on seventeen to close to within two strokes of Robbins.

Cherry's approach shot on the final hole finished fifteen feet from the cup. With little effort, the crooner made his putt for birdie. The pressure was now on the Memphis native who was left with a treacherous 20-inch putt for par. After careful study and a stroke of his putter, Hillman Robbins added the Sunnehanna Amateur trophy to his mantle. Robbins had demonstrated an uncanny ability to come from behind. At Memphis State, Robbins had come from behind in similar fashion to win both Southern Intercollegiate and National Intercollegiate titles.

Hillman Robbins victory was a considerable boost to the reputation of the Sunnehanna Amateurs. In only two years, the tournament had two national caliber champions that helped legitimize the Sunnehanna Amateur with golfers throughout the country.

Sunnehanna Amateur
GENE DAHLBENDER

*T*he prior summer, Sunnehanna Amateur Chairman, A.H. Wagner, and Club President Charles Kunkle, sowed the seeds for the tournament's continued improvement at the 1955 US Amateur. Played at The Country Club of Virginia in Richmond, Virginia, Kunkle, a participant who reached the quarter-finals, and Wagner met with the press, and members of the USGA.

'56

More importantly, they met with contestants, promoting the Sunnehanna Amateur. The feedback from the players was overwhelmingly positive. Many of the nation's top amateurs responded to Wagner's and Kunkle's efforts, accepting invitations.

Gene Dahlbender

Previous champions, Hillman Robbins and Don Cherry could not participate. Robbins had been inducted into the military, a common occurrence for college-aged men. Cherry had a conflict with a singing engagement. In spite of their absence, the Sunnehanna Amateur's field in 1956 was exceptional

The most accomplished contestant from the U.S. Amateur that Wagner and Kunkle persuaded to play in Johnstown was Bill Hyndman. Hyndman reached the finals, losing to Harvie Ward, the pre-eminent amateur in the country. The Huntington Valley, Pennsylvania golfer reached the finals defeating Joe Campbell in the quarter-finals and Sunnehanna Amateur champion Hillman Robbins in the semi-finals.

Other prominent players who accepted invitations included Dr. Ed Updegraff, the three-time Arizona Amateur and two-time Southwestern Amateur champion, from Tuscon, Arizona and Don Bisplinghoff, the 1955 North and South Amateur champion and three-time Florida Amateur champion. LSU standouts Eddie Merrins, a native of Meridian, Mississippi and Western Amateur champion, and Johnny Pott, from Eunice, Louisiana further strengthened the field.

A late addition to the Sunnehanna Amateur field was Jack Nicklaus. His invitation was the result of a letter from Bill Campbell. The playing captain for the 1955 U.S. Walker Cup team, Campbell, expressed regret in being unable to participate, but recommended the 16-year-old golfer. The previous summer, Nicklaus qualified for the U.S. Junior and U.S. Amateur and won

Schoolboy Shoots Six Birds, Eagle

Fifteen-year-old Jack Nicklaus of Columbus, Ohio, whose golf game looks more like that of a seasoned campaigner than of a high school junior, set tongues wagging Wednesday as he tuned up for the Sunnehanna Tournament of Amateur Champions.

Getting his first look at the hilltop course, Nicklaus plunked in six birdies and an eagle. But there is a sad part to the story. The youth made three visits to sand traps, where he lost six strokes, and had to settle for a two-over par 74. He bagged his eagle on the long par-5 dogleg No. 11.

Approximately one-third of the 36-man field entered in the 72-hole medal play event checked in Wednesday and promptly got into their work togs for a practice round. Only a few scores were reported, with the best being a 69 credited to Tim Holland of Rockville Center, N. Y.

the prestigious National Jaycees title, the top junior tournament in the country.

The tournament attracted coverage from newspapers such as *The New York Times*, *Philadelphia Inquirer*, *Pittsburgh Post-Gazette* and *Pittsburgh Sun-Telegraph*.

Jimmy Mann, editor for Golf World, the leading golf weekly, traveled from Pinehurst to cover the event.

Fred Byrod of the *Philadelphia Inquirer* wrote about the Sunnehanna Amateur's success in establishing a tournament free of a Calcutta and its value to greater Johnstown.

Bob Drum, who covered the Sunnehanna Invitational for the *Pittsburgh Press*, was effusive in his praise of the Sunnehanna Amateur and its medal play format. Drum wrote, "If the Sunnehanna people can continue to promote this affair, it will be the best amateur tournament in the world in the next ten years."

The print reporting was matched by television and radio coverage as both CBS and NBC devoted national weekend coverage and updates.

As for the tournament, Bill Hyndman of Philadelphia led by two strokes after rounds of 68-68-69. A final round of 76 by the 54-hole leader gave Gene Dahlbender the opening he needed. Dahlbender's final round of 69, added to his prior rounds of 71-67-69, broke Don Cherry and Hillman Robbins previous record total by four strokes. It was Dahlbender's second victory of the year, having won the Dogwood Invitational in the spring. Dr. Ed Updegraff and Robert Brownell from Duke University finished tied for third, six strokes behind the winner.

Jack Nicklaus shot a four round total of two-under par 286 with rounds of 72-72-72-70 to finish in fifth place, ten strokes behind the champion. He left a lasting impression on the spectators, members, and participants. Dr. Bob Reilly, who played with Nicklaus the first day,

Committee member, Wally Williams (right) points out a tricky pin position to Eddie Merrins and Tim Holland on his right. Howard Picking, Sunnehanna President , looks on.

recalled, "He was very impressive for a sixteen year-old. His concentration and dedication astounded me."

Nicklaus' prodigious length and the concept of plumb-bobbing, which hadn't been seen before attracted large crowds throughout the week. The attention was justified. In a few years he was on his way to becoming arguably the greatest player in the history of the game. Jack Nicklaus' participation in the

Mike Wolfe helps with the scores while brother Doug Wolfe admires the trophies. Twenty-three years later Doug Wolfe played in the Sunnehanna Amateur.

Sunnehanna Amateur became an indelible part of the tournament's rich history.

Gene Dahlbender accepted his invitation two days before the tournament started. Little was known about his considerable reputation in the east. Afterward, the 32-year old unknown Atlanta, Georgia native told the scribes about his successes in 1948 when he won the Southern Amateur and reached the semi-finals of the US Amateur. The next year Dahlbender turned professional joining, Claude Harmon's staff at Winged Foot in 1949. A year later he applied for the reinstatement of his amateur status, which was granted after a two-year probationary period in 1952.

The 1956 Sunnehanna Amateur was the most significant year in the tournament's history. A field of unquestionable quality was played in front of and reported by major media outlets. The committee couldn't have asked for a better way to promote the tournament to the nation's leading golfers and build on its remarkable success.

Sunnehanna Amateur
Recollections of Charley Nicklaus

Reprinted from the 1963 Sunnehanna Amatur program.
These are Charley Nicklaus' personal memories of Sunnehanna.

Dr. Bob Reilly, Jack Nicklaus and Tommy Lott

JACK NICKLAUS is one of many of today's great golfers who stopped at Sunnehanna Country Club on the way to the top. While Nicklaus, who was only a 16- year-old at the time, has only dim recollections of his play here, Charley Nicklaus, the young-at-heart father of the champion, recalls it vividly.

"1 had to be the chauffeur in those days," said the elder Nicklaus, "and that tournament was one I regret- ted only getting to once. It's funny how we arrived there as, being from Columbus, we were concentrating on Ohio tournaments at the time. I had vaguely heard of a good medal play tournament being held in Johnstown, Pennsylvania, but never having been tendered an invitation, I figured it was only for the big ama- teurs.

"One night the phone rang and I answered it. The caller said I probably didn't know him but his name was Bill Campbell and he was a golfer who had played with Jack.

"'1 certainly have heard of you, Mr. Campbell,' I replied. 'I think everyone has heard of the captain of the Walker Cup team.' That sort of put him at ease and he started talking.

"'I admire the way your boy plays the game,' said Campbell, 'and I would like to get him an invitation to play in the Sunnehanna Tournament of Champions. Would Jack like to play?

"'Certainly,' was all I said, and that's how it came about. Imagine Bill Campbell thinking that nobody had ever heard of him.

"Jack finished 5th that year [1956], but he was in some tough competition. Johnny Pott, Ed Tutwiler, Bill Booe, Don Bisplinghoff and Gene Dahlbender were some of the names in the field. In fact, I think Dahlbender set the record that year with a 276." [He did - and broke it four years later with a 273.]

"Jack didn't do anything spectacular - he scored even par the first three rounds. The last day he had a chance to do something as he made an eagle at the short par five on the front nine (six) and was four under par at one time. He managed a 70 and I was mighty proud of him finishing fifth. After all, he was only 16 years old." Nicklaus never came back to Sunnehanna, but that's another story Charley likes to tell. "I had made up my mind that Sunnehanna was one place I would want to return to, especially since it had a medal play format, something which Jack rarely competed in, as most amateur tournaments were match play.

"But every year from that point, Jack qualified for the National Open and he felt that he should practice the week before the Open rather than compete.

"I still see the invitations coming here year after year with a personal note from Charley Kunkle, asking us to attend. It was hard for me to turn down the invite year after year, but I had to. After all, Jack has always been the boss of his actions on the course. One year, I even told him he was depriving me of a good time because I really enjoyed myself there.

"All he said was to learn how to play a little better and I might get an invitation myself. I never did get my game in that good a shape, however.

"Well, we are going to quite a few places now, so I guess everything evens up. You know, though, I'd like to go back to Sunnehanna once more with Jack. I think he would have a helluva chance to win."

Sunnehanna Amateur
JOE CAMPBELL

Champions from throughout the country accepted invitations to compete in the 1957 Sunnehanna Amateur.

'57

Dr. George Wheeling, Club President, presents Joe Campbell, center, with the champion's trophy. Runner-up Bobby Pratt shares in the ceremony. Dr. Wheeling was a civic leader and a strong supporter of golf and the Sunnehanna Amateur.

Included in the field was 1956 champion Gene Dahlbender and runner-up Bill Hyndman. The committee invited ninety players, including golfers from Canada, England and Mexico, 40 players from 29 states accepted invitations.

One player received the largest share of the pre-tournament attention: Joe Campbell.

A likely member of the 1957 US Walker Cup team after reaching the semi-finals in the 1956 U.S. Amateur, Campbell returned to Johnstown after a one-year absence.

The native of Anderson, Indiana, Campbell dominated amateur golf in the Hoosier state winning three straight Indiana Amateur titles and two Indiana Junior and Open championships. Six of those titles came in 1955 and 1956 as Campbell won the Indiana Junior, Indiana Amateur and Indiana Open titles in the same year.

After finishing fourth in the Sunnehanna Amateur in 1955, Campbell won the NCAA title and reached the quarter-finals of the U.S. Amateur. A two-sport star at Purdue, he was a starting guard on the basketball team.

Another notable player was Jennings "Jay" Randolph who won the Egyptian Amateur while stationed overseas. The son of United States Senator Jennings Randolph, Randolph played in the inaugural tournament in 1954. Then a 19-year-old from Washington D.C., Randolph had played in several national amateurs and was a standout player in the metropolitan Washington area.

At the conclusion of Friday's round, University of Houston golfers Phil Rogers and Jim Hiskey, and Dr. Ed Updegraff were tied for the lead with rounds of two-under par rounds of 68.

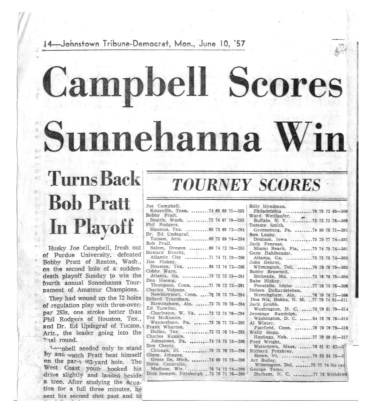

14—Johnstown Tribune-Democrat, Mon., June 10, '57

Campbell Scores Sunnehanna Win

Turns Back Bob Pratt In Playoff

Husky Joe Campbell, fresh out of Purdue University, defeated Bobby Pratt of Renton, Wash., on the second hole of a sudden-death playoff Sunday to win the fourth annual Sunnehanna Tournament of Amateur Champions.

They had wound up the 72 holes of regulation play with three-over-par 283s, one stroke better than Phil Rodgers of Houston, Tex., and Dr. Ed Updegraf of Tucson, Ariz., the leader going into the final round.

Campbell needed only to stand by and watch Pratt beat himself on the par-4 403-yard hole. The West Coast youth hooked his drive slightly and landed beside a tree. After studying the situation for a full three minutes, he sent his second shot past and to

TOURNEY SCORES

Joe Campbell, Knoxville, Tenn. ....74 69 69 71—283	Billy Hyndman, Philadelphia ....70 78 72 80—300
Bobby Pratt, Seattle, Wash. ....72 74 67 70—283	Ward Wettlaufer, Buffalo, N. Y. ....75 72 75 78—306
Phil Rodgers, Houston, Tex. ....68 73 69 72—284	Tommy Smith, Greensburg, Pa. ....74 80 76 71—301
Dr. Ed Updegraf, Tucson, Ariz. ....68 73 69 74—284	Bob Leahy, Denison, Iowa ....75 75 77 74—301
Bob Prall, Salem, Oregon ....69 74 72 70—285	Jack Penrose, Miami Beach, Fla. .....75 74 78 74—301
Howard Everitt, Atlantic City ....71 74 71 70—286	Gene Dahlbender, Atlanta, Ga. ....75 75 78 74—302
Jim Hiskey, Houston, Tex. ....68 72 74 72—286	John Gehret, Wilmington, Del. ......70 78 76 79—303
Cobby Ware, Atlanta, Ga. ....73 72 73 73—291	Bobby Brownell, Bethesda, Md. .....73 76 76 79—304
Don Hoenig, Thompson, Conn. ....71 76 72 72—291	Babe Hiskey, Pocatello, Idaho ....77 78 75 76—306
Charles Volpone, Newburyport, Conn. .....70 76 73 75—294	Nelson DeBardeleben, Birmingham, Ala. ....76 79 76 75—306
Dillard Traynham, Birmingham, Ala. ....73 75 70 76—294	Don Nix, Hobbs, N. M. ..77 79 74 81—311
Ed Tutwiler, Charleston, W. Va. .....72 72 74 76—294	Jack Grubb, Washington, D. C. .....75 79 81 79—314
Ted McKenzie, Waynesboro, Pa. ......75 76 71 73—295	Jennings Randolph, Washington, D. C. .....84 78 76 76—314
Frank Wharton, Dallas, Tex. ....72 73 76 74—295	Al Winter, Fairfield, Conn. ....78 79 79 79—316
Charles Kunkle, Johnstown, Pa. ......74 74 75 73—296	Wally Hopp, Hastings, Neb. ....77 79 80 81—317
Don Cherry, Chicago, Ill. ....70 75 76 75—296	Fred Wright, Watertown, Mass. ....78 81 81 82—3..
Glenn Johnson, Gross Ile, Mich. ......74 69 75 78—296	Richard Presbrey, Stowe, Vt. ....79 82 84 78—3..
Steve Caravello, Madison, Wis. ......78 74 72 74—298	Art Butler, Wilmington, Del. ......73 77 74 No car
Dick Semple, Pittsburgh .73 79 71 76—299	George Toms, Durham, N. C. ....77 78 Withdrew

Saturday's second round was washed out and required 36 holes of golf to be played on Sunday. After three rounds of play, Dr. Ed Updegraff led Phil Rogers by one stroke and Campbell by two strokes.

After seventy-two holes of golf, Campbell and Bobby Pratt, another University of Houston golfer from Seattle, Washington were tied, 71 and 70 respectively to pass Updegraff, who shot 74, and Rogers who shot 72.

The tie required the first playoff in the tournament's history. On the second playoff hole, Campbell safely reached the green in two shots and stood back and watched as Pratt beat himself. After his tee shot came to rest close to a tree, Pratt failed to recover and finished the hole with a double-bogey. With a routine par, Joe Campbell became the fourth champion of the Sunnehanna Amateur.

Joe Campbell (with hat) being congratulated by runner-up Bobby Pratt.

Sunnehanna Amateur
BILL HYNDMAN

*T*he 1958 Sunnehanna Amateur could not match the off-season for excitement. The tournament came under the scrutiny of the United States Golf Association. In October of 1957. Howard Picking, the Club president, received a letter of inquiry from Joe Dey, Executive Director of the USGA, regarding special benefits for players.

'58

Any benefits given to a player and the assumption of any costs were a violation of the Rules of Golf as they pertained to the definition of an "amateur golfer". A violation of the rules could lead to a player losing his amateur status.

Bill Hyndman

The Club turned the issue over to Charles Kunkle who handled communications with Dey and the USGA. Kunkle and the tournament committee understood the significance of the inquiry. Dealing quickly with the maelstrom was important to the tournament's future. Top players legitimate concerns about jeopardizing their amateur status could adversely impact the tournament.

Kunkle explained that a larger field than previous years and the reluctance of some members to house married contestants led to a housing shortage. The committee was forced to utilize the Stanwix Hotel for six contestants. Kunkle acknowledged the tournament's assumption of hotel costs and, in prior years, caddy fees as well, both violations of the Rules of Amateur Golf. He also addressed another issue of concern for the USGA: the $20 entry fee.

The six players, whose rooms were paid for, were notified of the issue and sent bills to remunerate the tournament for the cost. Kunkle also reassured the USGA that the players were not responsible for the transgressions to insure that their amateur standing was not jeopardized.

By April, the USGA was satisfied that other outstanding issues were resolved and reached an understanding about the entry fee, which was raised to $25.

While the questions were resolved as far as the USGA was concerned, convincing the players was another matter. Joe Campbell had

not yet turned professional, but declined to return due to rumors about the return of the Calcutta.

Tommy Aaron remained concerned about participating as rumors persisted. A personal letter from Kunkle to Aaron attempted to address his concerns. All invitees were sent a two-page letter of facts using excerpts from the correspondence between the Kunkle and the USGA to satisfy player questions.

The committee also made the decision to reduce the size of the field to better manage the housing issue and avoid any potential problems.

P.J. Boatwright, a former Carolina's Amateur and Open champion, who was active in the Carolina's Golf Associations, accepted an invitation to play. His participation would later provide golf's ruling body a better understanding of how the tournament operated when he became Executive Director of the USGA.

As for the tournament, after three days of play, Bill Hyndmann, the recently crowned Philadelphia Amateur champion, claimed the title defeating Ed Brantly by one stroke and making his final-round collapse two years earlier a memory.

In October, the Board of Governors of Sunnehanna Country Club approved the scheduling of the Sunnehanna Amateur as an annual event until such time as it may be rescinded. While the tournament lost money, at that time $1000 a year, the Board believed that the overwhelmingly positive publicity the Club received, locally and nationwide, far outweighed the modest financial loss.

The Sunnehanna Amateur attracted large crowds.

Charles Kunkle, Jr.
Founder of the Sunnehanna Amateur

Charles Kunkle, founder of the Sunnehanna Amateur, competed in his final Sunnehanna Amateur in 1958. A fourth place finisher in 1954, Kunkle's playing ability and knowledge of the game was an incredible asset in the formative years of the Sunnehanna Amateur. The 1950 Sunnehanna Invitational champion, Kunkle qualified for five straight U.S. Amateurs beginning in 1954. His success in national amateur competition coincided with the birth of the Sunnehanna Amateur. The relationships and friendships he fostered at tournaments were crucial in the Sunnehanna Amateurs development. They accelerated the tournament's ascension to be among the nation's elite amateur tournaments.

In 1955, Kunkle reached the quarter-finals of the National Amateur earning him an invitation to the following year's Masters tournament. His success in the U.S. Amateur was a highlight in his amateur career, but the tournament was equally significant for the Sunnehanna Amateur. Hugh Wagner, Sunnehanna Amateur Chairman, and Kunkle spent time actively pursuing contestants for next years Sunnehanna Amateur. Ed Updegraff recalled, "After Charlie beat me in the round of 16, he encouraged me to come to Johnstown." The next year many of the tournament's top players traveled to Johnstown including Updegraff and another Kunkle opponent, Billy Booe, who beat Kunkle in the quarter-finals.

Kunkle's participation in the 1956 Masters also proved to be beneficial for the Sunnehanna Amateur. Bill Campbell, the playing captain of the 1955 U.S. Walker Cup team, took time to address the assembled golfers attending the amateur dinner. Kunkle recalled, "In the middle of dinner Bill Campbell stood up and said, 'I want all of you to play in my friend Charlie Kunkle's tournament. It's the best amateur tournament around.' " Campbell later aided the tournament by championing a young golfer from Columbus, Ohio to the committee. His name was Jack Nicklaus.

Kunkle was also a city tennis champion and high school basketball star at Westmont-Upper Yoder High School and then Duke University. After a tennis injury, Kunkle picked up the game of golf. The former captain of the Duke Basketball team, Kunkle's influence on golf at Sunnehanna Country Club and in Johnstown is epic. After the termination of the Sunnehanna Invitational, he continued to keep tournament golf alive at Sunnehanna, actively soliciting other events. In June of 1953, Kunkle proposed holding the Pennsylvania State Amateur, which was approved and held in 1955. He also discussed the possibility of starting another tournament with a variety of alternatives. These discussions ultimately lead to the reintroduction of tournament golf and the Sunnehanna Amateur. President of the West Penn Golf Association in 1963, Kunkle was also instrumental in the organizing the Greater Johnstown Golf Association.

Kunkle continued to serve as an active member of the Sunnehanna Amateur committee for forty-five years. His modest proposal fifty years ago quickly evolved into one of amateur golf's finest traditions and forever changed the face of amateur golf.

Howard M. Picking presents a plaque dedicating the first hole to Charles Kunkle, Jr.

ROBERT TYRE JONES, JR.
1425 C. & S. BANK BLDG.
ATLANTA, GEORGIA

May 8, 1959

Mr. Charles Kunkle, Jr., Tournament Chairman
Sunnehanna Country Club
Sunnehanna Drive
Johnstown, Pennsylvania

Dear Charlie:

You certainly have written me a very nice letter which makes me terribly sorry that I cannot attend your tournament.

I am sure you do not realize and cannot appreciate how difficult it is for me to even go through the usual motions of living away from home, not to mention travel or moving around a golf course in a gallery. Augusta simply is the only place where I can manage it. Many thanks to you anyway.

With best regards,

Sincerely,

Bob

RTJ:jsm

Sunnehanna Amateur

TOMMY AARON

Before play began for the fifth Sunnehanna Amateur title the 26 entrants who came from 22 states participated in the first Sponsor-Amateur tournament.

In response to the complaints about being unable to play the course for four days, Julius "Judy" Eckel proposed the concept of members playing a round of golf with a contestant. The Sponsor Amateur mirrored the professional tour's pro-am played prior to the tournament. This simple idea was enthusiastically received by the club's members and remains an integral part of the week's activities. Eckels proposal was a result of an off season which found the tournament's future in doubt.

Parker Lawson, Club President, Tommy Aaron, and future champions Ed Updegraff and Roger McManus

While the tournament was recognized nationally as a great success, some members resented the intrusion on their regular golf games and sacrificing the course for four days. They became vocal opponents of the tournament and eventually the Club's Board of Governors acknowledged their complaints. The tournament and its future was placed on the Board's monthly agenda.

Dean Beman won two U.S. Amateurs and won British Amateur title. He served as Commissioner of the PGA Tour for twenty years and oversaw its explosive growth.

Initially the opposition had the upper hand as two members of the Board were already outspoken critics of the event. A lively debate ensued, and the tournament's future seemed in doubt when an unexpected ally spoke. Charles Kunkle recalled Andy Fisher, the soft spoken General Manager of Bethlehem Steel, spoke directly to the matter: "I think that the golf tournament is a very good thing for this club. In the first week of June the golf course, the clubhouse, and every facility is in first class shape. After the tournament, the members have a country club that is in peak condition for the remainder of the year." Little was said in response to Fisher's comments. A vote was taken and by unanimous consent the Sunnehanna Amateur continued.

With another hurdle out of the way, the committee focused on attracting the nations best players to Sunnehanna.

The top entrants were Walker Cup teammates Deane Beman and Tommy Aaron.

Sunnehanna Amateur

Beman, a standout golfer from the University of Maryland, had just defeated Bill Hyndman, 1958 Sunnehanna Amateur champion, in the finals of the British Amateur and qualified for the U.S. Open.

Aaron, a native of Gainesville, Georgia and a collegiate golfer at University of Florida, lost in the finals of the 1958 U.S. Amateur to Charlie Coe. He had won back-to-back Southeastern Conference championships in 1957 and 1958.

Their achievements made them the favorites especially after the withdrawal of defending champion, Bill Hyndman, who withdrew exhausted after two weeks of competitive play in Great Britain.

After three rounds, Aaron was five strokes ahead of perennial contender, Ed Updegraff . Aaron opened the tournament with 67 and added scores of 66 and 71.

The final day, Updegraff played the first five holes in one-under par and shrank the Georgia native's five-stroke margin too two strokes. On the eighth tee it looked as if Aaron had provided Updegraff the opportunity to get even closer. The leader hit a wayward tee shot that ended up in the trees. From an awful position, Aaron hit a miraculous recovery shot. The ball eluded the outstretched tree branches, skipped out of a greenside bunker and onto the green. He escaped with a fortunate par and his lead.

Having averted a major disaster, Aaron played the next ten holes in even par which Updegraff could only match. On eighteen, Aaron finished in spectacular style; his approach shot finished less than a foot from the pin before a crowd estimated in excess of 1500 spectators. Later, the newly crowned champion admitted playing well but admitted, "I got the breaks."

Updegraff finished in second three strokes behind the winner followed by Roger McManus who was a distant third, seven strokes behind Updegraff. As for Beman, obviously weary from his travels, a final round of 69 tied him for fourth place.

At the opposite end of the scoreboard from Tommy Aaron was Charles "Chick" Evans. Evans was the first amateur to capture the U.S. Open and Amateur titles in the same year (1916). It is an accomplishment matched only by the great Bobby Jones. Evans added another Amateur title to his remarkable resume in 1920 defeating another amateur legend, Francis Ouimet. Evans attracted large galleries all week, recounting on countless stories and recollections of golfs greatest players with the spectators.

His achievements in golf were eclipsed by the establishment of the Evans Scholarship program. The Evans Scholarship became the largest privately funded scholarship program in the country assisting more than 7,000 caddies attend college.

Known as the "Grand Old Man", Evans participated in tournaments, like the Sunnehanna Amateur, as a goodwill ambassador for the game. The Sunnehanna Amateur enriched by his presence and legacy.

Sunnehanna Amateur

GENE DAHLBENDER

Four members of the victorious 1959 US Walker Cup team were among the 37 contestants entered in the 1960 Sunnehanna Amateur. The four players defending Sunnehanna Amateur champion Tommy Aaron and former champion Bill Hyndman were joined by Ward Wettlaufer, the 1958 Eastern Amateur and semi-finalist in the US Amateur champion, and playing captain, Bill Campbell.

Tournament veterans, Ralph Bogart, Roger McManus, Ed Tutwiler, and Ed Updegraff returned as well. The continuity these players provided resulted in strong personal friendships with members that lasted lifetimes. Their participation enhanced support for the tournament, as the members looked forward to rekindling their friendships for a few days each summer. They were also invaluable in promoting the tournament to amateur golfers throughout the nation.

Entering the tournament at the last minute, again, was former champion, Gene Dahlbender. Dahlbender returned to Johnstown after failing to qualify for the US Open.

When play began, more than one-third of the players broke par and seven others equaled par the first day. Juan Antonio Estrada from Durango, Mexico and Dick Crawford, the National Intercollegiate champion from the University of Houston led the assault on par with rounds of six-under par 66. One shot behind was Gene Dahlbender and Jack Rule, the Iowa Amateur champion.

Gene Dahlbender entered the final round with a six-shot lead over his closest competitor after superlative rounds of 67-67-66. With nine holes to play, Ed Updegraff cut his lead in half. It was as close as Updegraff would get, finishing three strokes behind and runner-up for the second consecutive year. Ralph Bogart and Juan Estrada finished in third, four strokes behind. The players endured rain, sleet, and snow the last day continuing a dubious tournament tradition with a seventh straight year of rain

Gene Dahlbender's record total of 273 was remarkable considering the weather. On the final green in regulation, Dahlbender attempted his final hole in a pounding rain. His first putt went only a few feet; his second putt went two-feet. He called it quits until the rain subsided and when he returned, the Atlanta, Georgia golfer took a seven-iron and lofted the ball the remaining 12 inches into the bottom of the cup. With his victory, Gene Dahlbender became the first two-time winner of the Sunnehanna Amateur.

Gene Dahlbender—The first two time champion of the Sunnehanna Amateur.

Sunnehanna Amateur

DICK SIDEROWF

Thirty-nine players representing twenty-four states and Mexico came to Johnstown for the eighth annual Sunnehanna Amateur.

While Gene Dahlbender did not return

'61

to defend his title, runner-

Dick Siderowf, Club President, Homer Chalfont, and Runner-up James Dolan

Jay Sigel competed in 23 Sunnehanna Amateurs. The first was in 1961.

up Ed Updegraff and third place finishers Ralph Bogart and little Juan Antonia Estrada, the Mexican Amateur champion from Torreon, Mexico, did return. Also returning was Richard Crawford, the two-time National Intercollegiate champion from the University of Houston.

The competitors again played a wet Sunnehanna golf course. After 54 holes were completed, Dick Siderowf was three strokes ahead of James Dolan, the first round co-leader.

In the final round, Siderowf, the two-time Connecticut Open and Amateur champion, carded his worst score of the tournament, 72, but held on to win by one stroke over Dolan, the Vermont Open champion.

The Sunnehanna Amateur was Dick Siderowf's first national amateur title. Siderowf later won two British Amateur titles (1973, 1976), the Canadian Amateur and the Northeast Amateur. In Connecticut, he won four Connecticut titles, three additional state amateur titles and an open championship to become one of the great players from the Nutmeg State.

Sunnehanna Amateur
DR. ED UPDEGRAFF

*T*he 1962 Sunnehanna Amateur included players who had won three Sunnehanna Amateur titles, three U.S. Amateur titles and two British Amateur .

Five players from the University of Houston journeyed to Johnstown. It was the first time an entire collegiate team participated in the tournament.

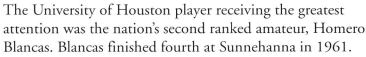

Dr. Ed Updegraff stands in front of his winning scores.

The University of Houston player receiving the greatest attention was the nation's second ranked amateur, Homero Blancas. Blancas finished fourth at Sunnehanna in 1961.

Also returning to Johnstown after a two-year hiatus was Deane Beman the 1960 U.S Amateur champion.

The first round leaders were a blend of something old, Bill Hyndman, and something new, Kermit Zarley from the University of Houston and Jay Sigel, the two-time Pennsylvania Junior and National Jaycees champion. Sigel was appearing in Johnstown for the second time, providing spectators a glimpse of the player who became the dominant face of the Sunnehanna Amateur over the next 30 years.

After Saturday's rounds, sentimental favorite Dr. Ed Updegraff stood one stroke ahead of 1958 champion Bill Hyndman and four clear of Blancas. Updegraff's

Homero Blancas, Jr. tied for second.

play on the back nine in each of Saturday's rounds was the difference.

In the morning round, he birdied the final four holes to shoot 31 and a sparkling round of 66. In the afternoon, Updegraff shot 69 aided by a back nine score of 32 that included four birdies. While Updegraff took advantage of the back nine, Hyndman imploded on his final nine coming home with a four-over par 39. Twice a runner-up at Sunnehanna, Dr. Ed Updegraff was 18 holes from capturing a title that had eluded him.

The final day started like the previous day had ended as Hyndman bogeyed the opening hole while Updegraff made a birdie. Updegraff finished the front nine with 34 and the title seemed assured. The Tuscon physician showed his partners how to play the inward nine making three consecutive birdies on eleven, twelve, and thirteen. His final margin of victory was five strokes over Bill Hyndman and Homero Blancas.

Dr. Ed Updegraff was a popular champion. Respected by players and members alike, no player or Sunnehanna Amateur champion represented the game and the tournament with more class. As a player, he made his first Walker Cup team in 1963 at the age of 41, in 1965, and finally at the age of 47 in 1969. In addition to the Sunnehanna Amateur, Updegraff's amateur record included the Southwestern, Pacific Coast, and Western Amateur titles as well as competing in 17 U.S. Amateurs.

Bill Hyndman, 1958 Champion, tied for second.

Winner Dr. Ed Updegraff receiving his trophy as Bill Hyndman looks on.

Sunnehanna Amateur
ROGER McMANUS

Lloyd Monroe, Roger McManus, Vinnie Giles and Bill Wilson

A modest field of 27 players entered the tournament in 1963. The field was weakened by several late withdrawals because the NCAA Championship started the day after Sunnehanna's final round. Dr. Ed Updegraff returned to defend his title so did 1961 champion Dick Siderowf.

Marvin "Vinnie" Giles of the University of Georgia led after the first round and was tied after 54 holes at 211 with Lloyd Monroe, the reigning New Jersey Amateur champion. Arizona State standout George Boutell was two behind and Roger McManus threes strokes back.

The final day, Giles who won the U.S. Amateur in 1972, struggled and shot a four-over par 39 on the front nine. While Giles stumbled, Roger McManus surged with four birdies on the same nine and shoot two-under par 33 to tie Monroe for the lead.

McManus took his first lead of the tournament with a three-foot birdie on the thirteenth hole only to be tied by an even shorter birdie on fifteen by Monroe. On the final hole, McManus and Monroe reached the green in regulation. After their first putts, McManus remained a foot from the cup and Monroe only a few inches. The Ohio native made his putt and the gallery anticipated a playoff. They then watched in disbelief as Monroe missed.

Roger McManus played in his fifth straight Sunnehanna Amateur in 1963. The career amateur from Hartsville, Ohio was a part of a core group of amateurs who were warmly welcomed back every year. The mild mannered McManus had a fine amateur record qualifying for seven straight U.S. Amateurs, reaching the semi-finals in 1958. The Sunnehanna Amateur was his only major amateur title.

Sunnehanna Amateur
GARY COWAN

Thirty players including defending champion Roger McManus and three former champions—Bill Hyndman, Gene Dahlbender, and Ed Updegraff—vied for the title.

Also returning was 1962 runner-up Homero Blancas who was on leave from military service.

Gary Cowan's first trip to Johnstown was memorable for many reasons. The 1962 World Amateur titlist from Kitchener, Ontario, Canada came to the Sunnehanna Amateur on his honeymoon. His tournament schedule had taken Cowan to Australia, South Africa, Mexico, Japan and the United States.

Gary Cowan receives the champion's trophy from Wayne Wolfe, President.

After three rounds, Bill Hyndman led Robert Reilly, the West Penn Amateur champion from Pittsburgh, by two strokes and Cowan by three strokes. The final round began poorly for the leader as Hyndman bogeyed three of the first four holes. He recovered with two birdies later on the front nine to share the lead with Reilly. Cowan was still three behind.

Cowan, the Low Amateur in the 1964 Masters, began the final nine making birdies on ten and eleven to take the lead as Hyndman and Reilly struggled. A par on fourteen by Cowan coupled with bogeys by Reilly and Hyndman widened the Canadian's lead. A birdie on fifteen wrapped-up the title.

The 1964 Sunnehanna Amateur title was Gary Cowan's first major amateur championship in the United States. Two years later, he captured his first U.S. Amateur title, defeating Deane Beman at Merion. In 1971 he won again at Wilmington Country Club beating Wake Forest standout, Eddie Pearce.

Bob Reilly, Bill Hyndman, Wayne Wolfe and Gary Cowan.

Sunnehanna Amateur
BOBBY GREENWOOD

*T*hirty-nine entries accepted invitations to compete for the twelfth Sunnehanna Amateur.

The previous four champions, Gary Cowan, Roger McManus, Dr. Ed Updegraff, and Dick Siderowf returned hoping to win a second title.

Dick Canon, Champion Bobby Greenwood, Club President Bob Smith, Dick Siderowf and Ed Tutwiler

Prominent returnees included Don Allen, the three-time New York Amateur champion and Bob Reilly, the four-time West Penn Amateur champion.

Paul Desjardins, a native of Miami Shores, Florida, led after the first round with an opening round of five under par 67. Desjairdins, the Mexican Junior champion, was one of three members of the University of Miami golf team in the tournament. Johnstown native and Sunnehanna member, Bill Crooks, and Jerry Potter, the Jamaican Amateur champion the other two. One stroke behind was Harry Toscano, the Pennsylvania Amateur champion from New Castle, Pennsylvania. The most interesting opening round story was Bobby Greenwood who shot 70. While his fellow contestants worked on their games and played practice rounds, Greenwood relaxed at the clubs pool. His clubs, shoes, and clothing had been lost in transit. With play about to begin and his clubs nowhere to be found, the Cookeville, Tennessee swinger was forced to find suitable replacements. He borrowed woods from club member, Jack Vanjo, irons from head professional John Goettlicher, and a putter from course superintendent Joe Harlow.

On the seventh tee on Saturday morning, Bobby Greenwood was reunited with his equipment. One under at the time, Greenwood kept Harlow's putter and switched to his own clubs and then played the next eleven holes in six under par. His seven under par round of 63 established a new competitive course record. It also put him in the lead by six strokes, a margin he maintained after an afternoon round of 70. First round leader Paul Desjardins and Ed Tutwiler were his closest pursuers.

On Sunday, golf enthusiasts who couldn't get to the course, tuned in and watched Greenwood and his pursuers on television. The final two holes were covered live by WJAC-TV. The television station's moniker "Serving Millions from Atop the Alleghenies", gave viewers throughout Central and

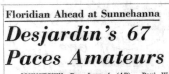

Floridian Ahead at Sunnehanna
Desjardin's 67 Paces Amateurs

JOHNSTOWN, Pa., June 4 (AP) — Paul W. Desjardins of Miami Shores, Fla., shot a three-under-par 35-32—67 Friday to take the opening round lead in the 72-hole Sunnehanna Amateur Golf Tournament.

Desjardins, the Mexican junior champion, had one birdie on the outgoing nine and three birdies and six pars coming in over the par 35-35-70, 6,683-yard course.

Gary Cowan of Kitchener, Ont., who won the tourney last year, finished far down in the field of 38. He shot a 40-34-74.

Harry Toscano, Jr. of New Castle, Pa., and Roger T. McManus of Hartville, Ohio, were the only other players to finish below par.

Toscano carded a 35-33-68 and McManus, who won the Sunnehanna championship in 1963, finished with a 37-32-69.

Dick Siderowf of Westport, Conn., also a former Sunnehanna champ, finished sixth with a 38-32-70.

Dr. E. R. Updegraff of Tuscon, Ariz., the winner of the

PAUL DESJARDINS
Junior out front.

Sunnehanna Amateur

Western Pennsylvania the opportunity to watch amateur golf's best players. During the final round viewers and spectators watched Bobby Greenwood continue his scintillating play firing a final round of 66. The North Texas State All-American's four-round total of 269 shattered Gene Dahlbender's 72-hole total set in 1960 by four strokes.

Lost in Greenwoods spectacular play was the impressive play of runner-up Dick Canon. Canon matched Greenwood over the final 54 holes with rounds of 67-67-65, but finished five behind the champion, a first round 75 too much to overcome.

A testament to Greenwood and Canons fine play was that only three other players managed to equal or break par. Third place finishers, Dick Siderowf and Ed Tutwiler were two-under par for the tournament, eight strokes behind the champion.

After the round, Greenwood had a new concern as he prepared to head home: Joe Harlow's borrowed putter. "Joe told me to keep it," he said. "Maybe I will."

Not only did Bobby Greenwood leave Johnstown with the winner's trophy, he packed the putter that helped make it possible.

Sunnehanna Professional John Goettlicher (in sunglasses) gets instructions on a new camera from Bill Wilson (right).

University of Miami teammates Jerry Potter and Sunnehanna member Bill Crooks

Sunnehanna Amateur

JACK LEWIS

Jack Lewis, the 1966 Sunnehanna Amateur champion, and runner-up Bob Murphy. Murphy, the 1965 U.S. Amateur champion, won the NCAA individual title in 1996. Both Lewis and Murphy were named to the 1967 U.S. Walker Cup team

One of the youngest and most accomplished fields in the tournaments history participated in the Tournament for Champions in 1966. The field of 41 players included four of the nation's top ten amateurs. Defending Sunnehanna Amateur champion Bobby Greenwood, 1965 U.S. Amateur champion, Bob Murphy, and Western Amateur champion Bob Smith, could be found preparing for three days of tournament play.

Also taking up temporary residence in Johnstown was Arizona State's George Boutell the nations top ranked amateur. In 1965, Boutell won the Trans-Miss and Eastern Amateur titles.

Boutell arrived with University of Houston star, Marty Fleckman. Fleckman won the 1965 NCAA championship and the 1964 Texas Amateur. A year later he led the 1967 U.S. Open at Baltusrol for three rounds.

A first time participant's invitation could be attributed to an Easter visit to Sunnehanna's pro shop. Dr. Fred Mehlhorn, a former resident of Johnstown, informed Sunnehanna's Head Professional John Goettlicher about a talented young player who played at his home club in Richmond, Virginia. He was the Virginia High School champion and two-time Virginia Junior champion, Lanny Wadkins, who had just finished his sophomore year in high school. Wadkins was invited and made the first of six trips to Johnstown.

The first-round leader was a familiar one, Ed Updegraff. Pre-tournament favorites Boutell, Fleckman, and Smith were joined by Jack Lewis, a freshman from Wake Forest College, one shot behind the leader.

The final day of golf shaped up to be a two-player tournament between Bob Murphy and Jack Lewis. Tied with a three-round total of 211, the next closest competitor was Ed Updegraff who was two strokes behind.

The final round found Murphy, who had won the Florida Amateur the week before, chasing the young Lewis. Birdies on eleven and thirteen by the Demon Deacon, followed by bogeys on fourteen and seventeen by Murphy, led to a four-shot victory for Jack Lewis.

Bob Murphy recovered from his disappointing final round winning the NCAA title at Stanford University two weeks later. Jack Lewis became the youngest champion in the history of the tournament and established himself as a player to watch the next several years at Sunnehanna.

Sunnehanna Amateur
BILL HYNDMAN

orty-two invitees accepted their invitations in 1967. The top eight finishers from the prior year returned including among them defending champion Jack Lewis, runner-up Bob Murphy, Marty Fleckman, Ed Updegraff, and Gary Cowan.

The first-round leader was 47-year old, Ed Tutwiler. The closest the genial former member of the U.S. Walker Cup team had come to winning the Sunnehanna Amateur was third in 1965. Tutwiler's round of 65 placed him three strokes ahead of 19-year old defending champion Jack Lewis and 18-year old Lanny Wadkins.

After the morning round on Saturday, Tutwiler was tied with Lanny Wadkins. Wadkins added a second round of 68 to his opening round of 67.

At days end on Saturday, Wadkins, Gary Cowan, and Ron Cerrudo stood two strokes ahead of veteran Dale Morey and three strokes ahead of Bill Hyndman.

Addressed by his younger playing partners prior to the final round as "Mister Hyndman," Bill Hyndman showed no signs of age in his game. A front nine of 32 put the respected veteran a stroke behind another former Sunnehanna Amateur champion, Gary Cowan.

A birdie on the sixteenth by "Mr. Hyndman" tied Cowan. Meanwhile, playing partner Lanny Wadkins launched a furious comeback on the back nine, closing within one stroke of the leaders. After barely missing a birdie on seventeen, Wadkins watched Cowan and Hyndman two putt from long distance on eighteen and then narrowly missed his birdie putt. He finished alone in third. Gary Cowan and Bill Hyndman needed extra holes to crown a new champion.

On the first playoff hole, Cowan and Hyndman reached the green in regulation. After Cowan narrowly missed his birdie putt, Bill Hyndman drained his, joining Gene Dahlbender as the second two-time champion of the Sunnehanna Amateur.

The victory was possibly the most important of Hyndman's career. His victory against an outstanding field re-invigorated his amateur career and put him on the short list for the next years Walker Cup team.

Bill Hyndman, 2nd from left, accepts his second Sunnehanna championship trophy from Club President, Charles Price. Lanny Wadkins, left, finished third, Gary Cowan, far right, lost in a play-off to finish second.

Ed Tutwiler Shoots 65, Leads Field by 3 Shots

Sunnehanna Amateur
BOBBY GREENWOOD

A record field of 50 contestants, surpassing the previous record of 42 players, met at Sunnehanna Country Club in June of 1968. Among the top returnees were defending champion Bill Hyndman, Jack Lewis and Lanny Wadkins.

'68

Also returning was Bobby Greenwood. Greenwood endured physical problems and mental mistakes after winning the tournament in 1965. In 1966, he was penalized four strokes for carrying two clubs too many and shot 81. In 1967, a broken wrist forced him to withdraw from the tournament.

Bobby Greenwood (left) won by one shot over Dr. Edgar Updegraff and Jack Lewis (right). Club President Gwynne Dodson looks on.

Among the acclaimed first time participants were Steve Melnyk and Billy Joe Patton.

Melnyk was a stand out player at the University of Florida. The Brunswick, Georgia native won seven tournaments including the Southeastern Conference title.

Billy Joe Patton's appearance in the Sunnehanna Amateur was long overdue. A five-time member of the Walker Cup team and three time winner of the North-South Amateur, Patton achieved national notoriety in the 1954 almost winning The Masters.

When play began, former champions Jack Lewis and Ed Updegraff quickly took charge opening with rounds of 66 to lead by four strokes.

After 54 holes another champion, Bobby Greenwood was in the lead by one stroke over Ed Updergraff and Bruce Ashworth.

The final day, Ashworth, a sophomore at the University of Houston, took the lead until Greenwood and Updergraff made birdies on fourteen, creating a three-way tie. Jack Lewis was one behind

On fifteen, Ashworth made the first of three bogeys to scuttle his title hopes. Greenwood, Updegraff, and Lewis reached the eighteenth green tied for the lead. After Lewis and Updegraff made par, Greenwood drained an eight-foot birdie putt to win the tournament.

The Cookeville, Tennessee native birdied three of the final five holes to win the tournament. With his dramatic putt on the final hole, Bobby Greenwood joined Gene Dahlbender and Bill Hyndman as two-time champions of the Tournament of Champions.

Sunnehanna Amateur
LEONARD THOMPSON

Twenty-nine contestants in the 43-player field were playing in their first Sunnehanna Amateur. Although Bobby Greenwood had turned professional, the tournament had an exceptional field that included six former champions.

Wake Forest standouts Lanny Wadkins (the Southern Amateur champion), and Jack Lewis; Florida State graduate and Birmingham, Alabama native, Hubert Green; University of Houston freshman, Jim Simons; and Steve Melnyk were all considered likely title contenders.

An opening round of 67 placed Jim Simons a single stroke ahead of University of Georgia standout and Southwestern Amateur champion, Allen Miller, Steve Melnyk, and Leonard Thompson. When Sunday arrived, Leonard Thompson led teammate Lanny Wadkins by a single stroke. His lead was the result of a Saturday afternoon round of 64 that included a record-tying score of 30 on the backside.

Thompson struggled early in the final-round. In spite of a front nine score of two-over-par 37, he remained one stroke ahead of Wadkins. Ahead of the final group, Hubert Green shot 32 (the low front nine score of the week) and picked up five strokes on the leader. The back nine began with birdies on ten by Thompson, Wadkins, and Green. On the easy eleventh, Thompson recorded the only birdie and widened his lead to two strokes.

Steve Melnyk was the nation's leading amateur in 1969. He won the 1969 U.S. Amateur and the Western Amateur. In 1971 Melnyk won the British Amateur.

Over the final seven holes, Thompson didn't miss a green, forcing his pursuers to make birdies to close the gap. Wadkins managed only one birdie on the final hole. Green gave himself a chance, making a birdie on seventeen, but his long birdie putt on the final hole didn't come close.

The 1969 Sunnehanna Amateur was the beginning of a major change in the tournament. It was the first time the cadre of career amateurs who had dominated the Sunnehanna Amateur leader board failed to finish in the top three. A new era began as college players captured 17 of the next 20 Sunnehanna Amateurs.

Leonard Thompson at the winners' table with William Price and Club President, Dr. Hampton Corson. Runner-ups Lanny Wadkins and Hubert Green look on. As a professional, Lanny Wadkins won 21 events, including the 1977 PGA title. Green won 19 times on tour. Green won two majors, the 1977 U.S. Open and the PGA title in 1985. Thompson won three PGA tour events.

Early American Amateur Golf

With the resurgence of interest in amateur golf, today's observers and players know little about amateur golf's past. The first 300 years of the game was the domain of amateur golfers. The National Open was won by amateurs Francis Quimet, Jerome Travers, Chick Evans and, later on, the great Bobby Jones.

The Depression and World War II ended the golden era of amateur golf, and post-war America shifted its attention to the professional game. As purses increased, colleges replaced the caddie as a breeding ground of talent for the professional tour. Players could also make a living without resorting to exhibitions to supplement their incomes as Hagen and Sarazen had before them.

In the 1950s and 1960s, amateurs were like many of their predecessors: educated, successful business men devoted to the game for the love of it. Amateur, the word comes from the Latin amare meaning "to love," appropri-

Dale Morey

ately describes the early amateurs and why they played the game. Amateur golf was still about friendly competition. Relationships forged between players and Sunnehanna members over the week of the tournament carried on beyond the course and lasted lifetimes. The players participated in many of the social activities that surrounded the tournament. Cocktail parties at member's homes abounded. Ed Updegraff, who participated in 15 of the first 17 Sunnehanna Amateurs, fondly recalled his times in Johnstown: "There was no other tournament like the Sunnehanna Amateur. The tournament competition was great, the people even better. The people involved with the tournament and

the members were interested in us as people not players. They treated us like family." As far as his fellow competitors, Updegraff remembers, "We had such great times with Bill Hyndman, Tut (Ed Tutwiler), Dale Morey. Roger McManus was one of the most wonderful people. They were great times and great people."

Ralph Bogart and Ed Tutwiler in 1963.

Updegraff, Bill Hyndman, Roger McManus and Ed Tutwiler were among the familiar friendly faces that returned every year. Gracious and friendly, they were also ambassadors for the tournament encouraging the nation's best players to travel to Johnstown.

They were also fine players.

Roger McManus

Bill Hyndman, a five-time member of the Walker Cup team, won the Sunnehanna Amateur twice and finished runner-up three times. The owner of a successful insurance agency in suburban Philadelphia, Hyndman was runner-up in the U.S. Amateur (1955) and British Amateur (1969 and 1970). Hyndman finally won a USGA title in 1973, the U.S. Senior Amateur, a title he won again in 1983 at the age of 67. Hyndman possessed a beautiful swing. Many of his victories were achieved at a late stage in most golfers' careers. He won his two Sunnehanna Amateur titles at the ages of 43 and 52, and the Northeast Amateur at almost 60. He was respected by many and showed a similar respect for others. Jay Sigel recalled Hyndman driving to Johnstown to watch the final round at Sunnehanna in 1976: "I noticed in the last round of the Sunnehanna that Bill Hyndman was out following me. We are both from Philadelphia and I have nothing but admiration for him and his record and here he was, out watching me. I wondered if I would do the same thing had the roles been reversed. That taught me something."

Ed Updegraff

Dr. Ed Updegraff, the 1962 Sunnehanna Amateur champion, was runner-up three-times, and like Bill Hyndman, improved with age. A weekend player, he made his first Walker Cup team at the age of 41 in 1963, again in 1965, and finally at the age of 47, in 1969. His teammates on that team included Steve Melnyk, Lanny Wadkins and Bruce Fleisher, all more than 25 years his junior. "It was an incredible feat to make the Walker Cup team at that age," said Melnyk. "He brought class, a level of character that was a wonderful addition, and strong playing characteristics." Bill Campbell, a Sunnehanna competitor, future USGA President and a member of the 1975 Walker Cup team which Updegraff captained, expressed nothing but admiration for Updegraff. "Nobody was ever more popular among players than Ed Updegraff, those who played with, against, and for him."

He played in his first Sunnehanna Amateur in 1956 and only missed one over the next 15 years. In 1999, the USGA honored Dr. Ed Updegraff by naming him the Bob Jones Award winner. Presented annually in recognition of distinguished sportsmanship, the USGA awards a person who emulated Bobby Jones' spirit toward the game and its players.

If there ever was a "King of Sunnehanna," Ed Tutwiler would have worn the crown. No player in the history of the tournament was as revered as "Tut". He never won the tournament; possibly his willingness to dance the night away or enjoy the evening cocktail parties had something to do with it. A native of West Virginia and lifelong friend of Bill Campbell and Sam Snead, he dominated amateur play in his home state. He later moved to Indianapolis, where he owned a successful Cadillac dealership. A participant in the inaugural "Tournament for Champions," Tutwiler played in 26 of the first 32 tournaments. In his final appearance in 1985, and well into his 60s, he shot one-under par 69. His best finishes were third in 1955 and 1971.

Talkative and funny, players of all ages and members were drawn to Tutwiler's quick wit and great sense of humor. In the 1959 tournament, his banter was noted by a reporter. Tutwiler, after accidentally topping his ball off the tee, quipped to the spectators, "It wasn't very far, but it certainly was straight." Chuckles and laughter ensued. Bobby Greenwood, in his first victory in 1965, commented afterward that Tutwiler's wisecracks kept him loose during his final round. A two-time member of the Walker Cup team, Tut lost to his good friend Bill Campbell, one-down in the finals of the 1964 U.S. Amateur. If ever a person represented the best of amateur golf, and love of the Sunnehanna Amateur, Ed Tutwiler was that person. Bobby Greenwood recalled, "Ed Tutwiler, Ed Updegraff, all of those guys were role models for us. They showed us how to act as young men. They were fine players and better people."

The list of other great amateurs surely would include Dick Siderowf, 1962 Roger McManus who the Sponsor-Amateur is named after, Billy Joe Patton, Ralph Bogart, Bill Campbell and Dale Morey, to name a few. Time has made these people a memory too many, but the qualities they exhibited on and off the course were the embodiment of what the founders of the Sunnehanna Amateur wanted when the tournament started.

Sunnehanna Amateur
HOWARD TWITTY

A record field of 65 players assembled at Sunnehanna's hilltop course to compete for the 17th annual title. Seven members of the

Howard Twitty, receiving the 1970 Sunnehanna Amateur trophy from Club President Fred Cunningham, later that year he won the Porter Cup. Accepting runner-up trophies are Lanny Wadkins (left) and Bob Clark (right).

winning U.S. Walker Cup team—Lanny Wadkins, Steve Melnyk, Dick Siderowf, Dr. Ed Updegraff, Allen Miller, Joe Inman and John Bohman—accepted invitations to play at Sunnehanna. Inman and Bohman made the team after former Sunnehanna Amateur participants Hubert Green and Bob Barbarossa declared their intention to turn professional.

Alternate Rick Massengale declined, as did Jack Lewis, Sunnehanna's 1966 champion who could not get out of summer classes at Wake Forest. This left Inman, the 1969 North and South champion, and Bohman, a third-place finisher in the 1968 U.S. Amateur, who accepted.

Out of eight first team NCAA All-Americans, five entered the tournament: Bob Clark, Howard Twitty, John Mahaffey, Wayne McDonald and Lanny Wadkins.

Three players owned national amateur titles: Steve Melnyk, the 1969 U.S. Amateur and Western Amateur champion; Wayne McDonald of Port Credit, Canada, the 1969 Canadian Amateur champion; and Christian Strenger from Cologne, Germany, the 1968 German and 1969 Swiss Amateur titlist. The USGA requested Strenger's invitation.

After the first round, Bob Clark, the 1968 NCAA champion from California State College at Los Angeles, led Leonard Thompson and Dick Siderowf by two strokes after an opening round of 65. Two rounds later, Clark continued to lead, his closest pursuer was Jerry Courville, the 1964 Northeast Amateur champion and former Connecticut Amateur and Open champion.

On the final day, Clark finished the back nine going bogey, double-bogey, bogey, relinquishing the lead to Courville. The Norwalk, Connecticut golfer maintained the lead until the twelfth hole. His second shot found a greenside bunker and he needed five strokes to get up and down from 15 feet.

His bunker shot bladed across the road ending in a clump of bushes 75 yards from the hole, ultimately leading to a triple-bogey seven. Courville's hopes of recovering from his debacle on twelve were extinguished by bogeys on two of the next three holes. After Courville's misadventure, Clark and Howard Twitty claimed a share of the lead.

Playing in front of the leaders was Lanny Wadkins who began the final round in twelfth place, eight strokes behind the leader. A third round of 66 got the Wake Forest star within shouting distance of the leaders after a slow start with rounds of 71 and a disheartening 76. A final-round front nine of 34 and three consecutive birdies to begin his final nine put Wadkins one stroke behind the leaders.

Howard Twitty, however, answered Wadkins valiant challenge making birdies on the thirteenth and fourteenth holes to take command of the tournament. Twitty's final round was nearly flawless making five birdies and one bogey to shoot a final round of 66, defeating Clark and Wadkins by three strokes.

The first major title of his career, Twitty's invitation was made possible after recommendations by Dr. Ed Updegraff and Bob Goldwater, a former Southwestern Amateur champion and brother of Barry Goldwater, Arizona Senator and 1964 Republican Presidential candidate. Twitty, the 1969 Western Amateur runner-up, later that summer added the Porter Cup title to his resume.

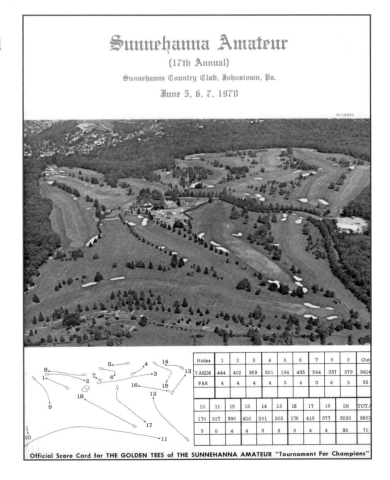

Sunnehanna Amateur

BOB ZENDER

*I*n 1971, the Sunnehanna Amateur welcomed back defending champion Howard Twitty, but the field was weakened by the success of members of U.S. Walker Cup team in the British Amateur.

The finals of golf's oldest amateur championship featured Jim Simons, and 1969 U.S. Amateur champion Steve Melnyk.

Melnyk's participation in the Walker Cup and subsequent success in the British Amateur was ironic. The USGA had suspended Melnyk from amateur competition for three months after receiving several dozen golf balls from a manufacturer.

Losing in the quarter-finals and semi-finals were Dr. Ed Updegraff and Tom Kite, respectively, further diluting Sunnehanna's field.

Only two members of the Walker Cup managed to get to Johnstown, Allen Miller and Lanny Wadkins both arrive the night before play began, surviving twenty-four hours of air travel.

Howard Twitty led the tournament after the first round with an opening round of 67. Trailing by two strokes was 1961 Sunnehanna Amateur champion, Dick Siderowf, and Canadian Amateur champion, Wayne McDonald.

The next day Bob Zender, the reigning Illinois Amateur champion, tied Bobby Greenwoods tournament record with a morning round of 63, putting him four strokes ahead of Stan Lee.

By days end, Zender stood two strokes ahead of his closest competitor, Rick Spears. A native of Port Jervis, New York, Spears picked up six strokes on the leader with an afternoon round of 67.

With one hole to play, Zender led the tournament by a single-stroke. His tee shot on the final went awry, finishing in the trees on the straightaway par four. After missing the green with his recovery shot, Zender hit a fine pitch shot leaving a four-foot putt for par. His putt to win the tournament failed to find the cup curling left just before the hole. Zender's bogey and Spears par forced the third playoff in the history of the event.

Both players made bogeys on the first playoff hole. On the second hole, Zender showed considerably better form, his approach shot finishing twelve-feet from the pin. Spear's first-hole struggles carried over to the second hole as his second shot missed the green and finished under the trees that framed the green. After pitching well past the hole, Spear's putt finished several feet past the cup. Zender, knowing Spear's plight, gently caressed his putt on the slippery green to a few inches, his par putt securing the title for the native of Skokie, Illinois.

Bob Zender with Club President, Byron Custer Jr. Zender defeated Rick Spears on the second playoff hole to win the tournament. In the second round, Zender tied Bobby Greenwood's single round tournament record shooting seven-under par 63.

Sunnehanna Amateur

MARK HAYES

The 1972 Sunnehanna Amateur had only nine contestants return from the prior year and included only one former champion, Roger McManus.

Among the noteworthy entrants were All-Americans Mark Hayes at Oklahoma State, Gary Sanders from USC, and University of Florida teammates Gary Koch and Andy North. Also competing in Johnstown for the first time was Atlantic Coast Conference champion Marty West from the University of North Carolina.

1972 Mark Hayes won three times professionally, the most prominent, being the 1977 Tournament Players Championship.

The most prominent returning player, after not competing the prior year, was Wake Forest's Jim Simons. In 1971, Simons was NCAA Player of the Year and after participating in the Walker Cup reached the finals of the British Amateur, losing to Steve Melnyk. The Butler, Pennsylvania natives most notable accomplishment in 1971 was his fifth place finish in the U.S. Open at Merion. Simons led the tournament by two strokes after 54 holes.

Mark Hayes, playing in only his second tournament in a year since joining the Army, led the tournament with an opening score of 66. A stroke behind was Joe Inman followed by Marty West and Bobby Wadkins two strokes back.

Jim Simons was considered one of the best amateurs in tournament.

Four strokes after the round, Hayes, a former two-time first team All-American at Oklahoma State, looked anything like the next champion early in the round, three putting the first and fifth holes for bogeys. Having missed the sixth green, and 90 feet from the hole, the prospects of another bogey by Hayes seemed likely. Then Hayes made a remarkable pitch shot from a horrendous lie. Clearing a bunker and landing 35-feet from the pin, his shot initially looked too strong. Then the pin and cup fortuitously got in the way. Hayes admitted, after his round, his amazing birdie won him the tournament. Hayes, steadied by his chip-in birdie, played solid golf over the final twelve holes and ended the tournament in style, his final approach finishing six-inches from the cup. His birdie tied the tournament record of 277 and defeated Marty West and Gary Koch by five strokes.

Mark Hayes had little time to celebrate his victory, the specialist fourth class was due back at Fort Jackson, South Carolina the next day.

Sunnehanna Amateur

BEN CRENSHAW

Golf fans throughout Western Pennsylvania were excited about the arrival of Ben Crenshaw in June of 1973. He was the best amateur golfer since Jack Nicklaus. In 1972 Crenshaw won the Porter Cup, Texas, Trans–Mississippi and Eastern Amateurs and shared the NCAA title with Longhorn teammate, Tom Kite. The Low Amateur in the 1972 and 1973 Masters, he had also won the Southern Amateur and NCAA titles in 1971.

Ben Crenshaw accepts the winner's trophy from Club President Robert Rose. Bobby Wadkins (left) finished third. Danny Edwards (far right) was runner-up. Edwards won five times on the PGA tour. Crenshaw won his first professional event, the Texas Open in 1973. As a professional, Crenshaw has won 19 times including the 1995 Masters.

Crenshaw's chief competition was expected to come from fellow All-Americans Danny Edwards of Oklahoma State, Gary Koch from the University of Florida, and Bill Rogers from the University of Houston.

After all the pre-tournament attention many felt that the next champion of the tournament was a foregone conclusion. Bill Rogers had obviously not read the papers and led at the completion of the first day's round with 66. Rogers denied Crenshaw's attempt to defend his Southern Amateur title in 1972. One stroke behind Rogers was Mike Killian, a former standout at the University of Florida. A large group of players were at even-par 70, including Bobby Wadkins, University of Georgia golfer David Canipe, and Gary Koch.

Crenshaw shot two-over par 72. After a front nine of 38, that included three bogeys and a double-bogey, the blonde Texan settled down and closed with an inward nine of 34.

Crenshaw's Saturday morning round of 68 was notable because of his score and a broken club. Responding to a wayward shot, Crenshaw displayed a temper more in keeping with "Terrible" Tommy Bolt than his nickname "Gentle Ben". Responding to an errant drive, he wrapped an iron around a tree until the head snapped off.

His second round on Saturday began with a front nine of three-over par 38. On the backside, Crenshaw was brilliant responding with birdies on the tenth, eleventh, twelfth, fourteenth, and eighteenth holes to shoot 30. Witnessing the birdie barrage Sunnehanna's golf professional, John Goettlicher, commented that Crenshaw could have shot 27 but missed three makeable putts.

With one round to play, Ben Crenshaw was the leader. Two-strokes behind Crenshaw was Danny Edwards. The 1972 North and South Amateur champion, Edwards scratched his way into second place with a morning round of 65 and an afternoon round of 71.

Sunnehanna Amateur

Bill Roger checks out his opening round score of 67. Rogers turned professional and won six events including the 1981 British Open title at Royal St. George's.

It was a two-player tournament and Danny Edwards closed the gap quickly making a birdie on the first hole. Crenshaw answered with birdies on the third and fourth holes as beautiful approach shots left him with modest putts of five feet and a foot to navigate for birdies.

Two strokes ahead after seven holes, Crenshaw hoped to avoid the hazards that existed on the tree-lined eighth hole. Earlier in the week, Crenshaw made a miraculous par from the weed-choked gully after an errant drive. Again, Crenshaw drove wildly into the trees on the right. Edwards responded with an equally poor drive of his own, which ricocheted among the trees to the left. Edwards failed to capitalize on Crenshaw's troubles making a bogey as the leader made a double-bogey. One hole later, Crenshaw showed the large crowd his famed putting stroke draining a 35-foot birdie putt to close the front nine with an even-par score of 35 to remain two strokes ahead of Edwards.

Edwards, a two-time first team All-American from Edmond, Oklahoma, wasn't about to quit as he pulled within one-stroke of Crenshaw with a birdie on fifteen. On the next hole, Edward's hopes of winning were dashed. A seemingly perfect approach skidded through the green ending precariously on the lip of the bunker. Unable to get his footing, Edwards stubbed his next shot and needed an additional two strokes to finish the hole.

A day of outstanding golf ended with Ben Crenshaw draining an 18-foot birdie putt on the final hole to shoot 67. Danny Edwards finished three strokes behind Crenshaw and Bobby Wadkins, finished third nine strokes behind the winner.

"I wanted to win a big one before the Open," said Crenshaw, "to have some confidence going into Oakmont. This is one of great amateur fields. I lost my cool the first day after such a poor start, and maybe what I did gave me a better mental attitude the rest of the way."

For Ben Crenshaw, it marked the beginning of an incredible summer. Over the next four months, he added a third NCAA title, a second Southern Amateur title, and the Northeast and Western Amateur trophies to his already crowded trophy case.

Crenshaw elected to forego his final season of eligibility at the University of Texas and turned professional that fall. At the tour qualifying school, he destroyed the field winning by twelve-strokes. Appropriately enough, he then won his first PGA event, the Texas Open. By any standard, Ben Crenshaw's performance in the summer of 1973 was one of the finest in the annals of amateur golf and remains the standard for any amateur golfer since.

Sunnehanna Amateur

DAVE STRAWN

The 1973 Sunnehanna Amateur field had only ten returnees from the previous year's tournament in its field of 53 players. The small group was led by Gary Koch from Temple Terrace, Florida. The Florida Gator had played well in his two previous appearances at Sunnehanna finishing fourth in the 1973 and runner-up in 1972.

Koch first appeared on the national golf scene in 1970 winning the U.S. Junior. Two years later he won the Florida Amateur. In 1973, Koch was a member of the winning Walker Cup team, won the Trans-Mississippi Amateur and finished second to Ben Crenshaw in the NCAA Championship.

Dave Strawn

Other players receiving pre-tournament attention were 1973 Walker Cup team members Marty West, the Middle-Atlantic and Maryland Amateur champion, and Mark Pfeil from USC. Fellow USC teammate Craig Stadler, the 1973 U.S. Amateur champion also came to Sunnehanna.

Wake Forest, the 1974 NCAA team champions, furnished the tournament with three outstanding players: Bob Byman, the three-time Colorado Amateur champion and 1972 U.S. Junior champion; Curtis Strange, the 1974 NCAA individual champion; and Jay Haas.

Before play began, George Burns received considerable media attention. Although a member of the University of Maryland golf team, Burns' game did not blossom until finishing school in 1972 when he won the 1972 Metropolitan Amateur and the 1973 Canadian Amateur title. In the spring of 1974, Burns added the Azalea and the North and South Amateur titles. He was the hottest player in amateur golf.

Burns opened the tournament with 67 to

Craig Stadler in modern attire and equipment. Stadler won the US Amateur in 1973. A seventeen time champion on the PGA tour, he won the Masters in 1982.

lead LSU standout Stan Lee by one stroke. Gary Koch, Oakmont's John Birmingham, and Don Allen were two-strokes behind.

A record of dubious distinction occurred during the first day's play, as John Hall of Duluth, Minnesota needed 11 strokes to traverse the 357-yard par 4 eighth hole. A topped tee shot into the famed gully was followed by a questionable decision to play from the overgrown abyss. That decision began his tale of woe. After extricating himself from the weeds, Hall made additional visits to several bunkers adding to his miasma and the ignominious double-digit score.

With one round to play, Burns continued to lead with Gary Koch, Marty West, and David Strawn a stroke behind. After a bogey on the fifth hole by Burns, all four players reached the sixth tee deadlocked. On the sixth hole, Burns made the second of four consecutive bogeys, which effectively eliminated him from contention.

As Burns, a soft drink salesman, fizzled-out, David Strawn took charge of the tournament. Strawn finished runner-up in four tournaments in 1973 the most notable runner-up finish was in the finals of the U.S. Amateur to Craig Stadler. A birdie on the relatively easy eleventh by Strawn, while Koch made a bogey, eliminated another competitor. The final pursuer, Marty West, was left in Strawn's vapor as the recent graduate of the University of South Carolina Law School added birdies on the twelfth, thirteenth and fifteenth holes. Strawn's lead was now an insurmountable four strokes with three holes to play.

The top three finishers all broke par on the final round. Both Koch and West shot 68, but David Strawn's back nine of 31, and final round of 65 gave him a well earned three-stroke victory over Gary Koch and Marty West.

Gary Koch, Champion Dave Strawn, Club President Dr. Barney Lovette, and runner-up Marty West

Sunnehanna Amateur
JAIME GONZALES

Sixty-two aspirants, the largest field in the tournament's history, came to Johnstown in quest of the coveted Sunnehanna Amateur title in 1975. The early favorites again came from the collegiate ranks.

Brigham Young's Mike Reid and Mike Brannan, as well as Jaime Gonzales, from Oklahoma State, and University of Florida teammates Phil Hancock and Andy Bean garnered most of the early attention. Hancock finished runner-up in the recently completed NCAA championships and fourth at Sunnehanna in 1974.

Jamie Gonzales won the tournament on the final hole sinking a 30-foot birdie putt to defeat Phil Hancock and Mike Reid by a shot. The 1974 World Amateur champion, Gonzales became the second foreign player to win the tournament.

No tournament had ever been shortened from 72 holes but torrential rains inundated the course on Friday making play impossible. The first round washout was disastrous for Mark Lye. The San Jose State star had played the first ten holes in three-under par only to see his efforts go down the drain.

After Saturday's double round, Jaime Gonzales, the 1974 World Amateur champion, was one stroke ahead of Phil Hancock and Mike Reid. A native of Rio De Janeiro, Brazil, Gonzales had reached the semi-finals of the 1973 British Amateur and played in the British Open. Opening the tournament with 71 in the morning, Gonzales added 67 in the afternoon, to take the lead. It was one of only two sub-par rounds.

The final round was played in abysmal conditions and only the hardiest spectators braved the elements to watch. With nine holes to play, Gonzales and Reid were tied and Hancock was three strokes behind. Hancock made a late bid with birdies on the thirteenth and fifteenth holes to tie him with Gonzales and get within one stroke of Mike Reid. A bogey on 17 by Reid resulted in a three-way tie going into the final hole.

All three players reached the eighteenth green in regulation where the 5'9", 120-pound Gonzales drained a dramatic 20-foot putt to give him his first major American amateur title.

The former first team All-American and Big Eight Conference champion came to Oklahoma State in 1973 barely able to speak English. One of three sons of a golf professional, his father worked at one of only two golf courses in Brazil. Gonzales had played in major amateur competitions throughout the world including England, Scotland, and South Africa, to name a few. He had never played in the United States until the Sunnehanna Amateur.

With his victory Jamie Gonzales, the eight-time Brazilian Amateur champion, became the second foreign champion of the Sunnehanna Amateur joining Gary Cowan.

Sunnehanna Amateur

JAY SIGEL

$\mathcal{A}$nother tournament's last minute decision to change its dates to correspond directly with the 1976 Sunnehanna Ama-

'76

teur significantly weakened the field. Taking advantage of the close proximity of the NCAA Championships being played at the University of New Mexico, the Southwestern Amateur moved the dates of its tournament with hope of attracting the best college players to their tournament. It worked.

In spite of the best efforts of chairman Bill Price, who was incensed by the change in dates, the tournament failed to attract any players from several of the nation's best college programs, notably Oklahoma State, Florida, and Wake Forest.

One school, Brigham Young, provided the Sunnehanna Amateur with three All-Americans: John Fought, the 1974 Pacific Coast champion; Jim Nelford, the 1975 Canadian Amateur champion; and Mike Brannan.

Playing in his tenth Sunnehanna Amateur was seven-time Pennsylvania Amateur champion Jay Sigel. Sigel had yet to win a major amateur championship.

The contingent from Brigham Young dominated the early rounds. An opening score of 65 put John Fought three strokes ahead of his closest competitor. Two rounds later, Mike Brannan, who was the 1970 U.S. Junior Champion, took the lead by a single stroke over Fought and Jay Sigel. After shooting his second consecutive round of 72, Fought quickly left the premises. The long hitting native of Portland, Oregon was annoyed after making bogeys on three of Sunnehanna's five par 3s.

On the final day, Brannan, the Western Collegiate champion, made bogeys on the second, third, and seventh holes and finished the front nine two strokes behind Fought and Sigel. Jay Sigel started the final nine with three consecutive birdies; it was the margin of difference between himself and runner-up John Fought. Mike Brannan finished in third, four strokes behind the winner.

"I tried to fight overconfidence after the three straight birdies," said Sigel. "I didn't have it won until the last hole."

Jay Sigel first appeared in Johnstown in 1961. After winning over 50 amateur golf titles, he added the Sunnehanna Amateur.

Jay Sigel won the first of three Sunnehanna Amateur titles. Brigham Young teammates John Fought and Mike Brannan finished second and third respectively. Fought won the US Amateur in 1977. He was the PGA Rookie of the Year in 1979. A neck injury forced Fought to leave the tour. He became a golf architect and designed Pumpkin Ridge with Bob Cupp which has held the US Amateur and US Woman's Open.

Sunnehanna Amateur

JOHN COOK

*T*he opportunity to be a member of the Walker Cup team was a prime motivator for 59 of the nation's best amateurs in 1977. The top finishers from the prior year returned to Johnstown including defending champion Jay Sigel. After the 1976 Sunnehanna Amateur, Jay Sigel added his eighth Pennsylvania Amateur title.

Champion John Cook (left) and Marty West

Also returning was John Fought, who won the Northwest Open and reached the quarter-finals of the U.S. Amateur, and Mike Brannan, who won his second California Amateur title.

Among the more prominent new players was Scott Simpson from U.S.C., the 1976 and 1977 NCAA champion, and Vance Heafner from North Carolina State, the 1976 Eastern Amateur champion.

Challenging winds and greens kept 58 of the 59 players grasping for birdies. Just as he did the year before, John Fought led after the first round. He was the only player to shoot a sub-par round on the first day with 69. A single shot back was Jay Sigel, Marty West, Gary Hallberg and Brigham Young teammate Pat McGowan.

Scott Simpson, the 1976 and 1977 NCAA Champion. Simpson won the US Open in 1987.

The morning round on Saturday, Fought, who later that summer won the U.S. Amateur, imploded with an uncharacteristic score of 78. The entire field failed to break par.

At the day's end on Saturday, John Cook, a first team All-American his freshman year at Ohio State, and Tom Evans, from Northbrook, Illinois were in the lead. A single stroke back was John Fought, as well as Hallberg, Heafner and West. Fought recovered from his morning debacle with an afternoon score of 66 to get back into contention. Scott Simpson, the reigning Porter Cup champion, was two strokes behind. The leader board was a testament to the quality of the field and the possibility of a terrific final day of play.

Gusty winds and a hard steady rain lashed the course and players on the final day. The miserable conditions diminished the quality of golf, as the players struggled with the conditions. On the ninth hole, Marty West stepped away from a putt to query the gallery, "I don't know why you people are here, you're nuts. I know why I'm here, I was told to be here."

Talk of an impending three-way playoff began after the combination of Marty West's birdie on eighteen and a bogey on seventeen by Cook tied both with Gary Hallberg. Determined to avoid a playoff, John Cook struck a brilliant 6-iron to two feet of the pin on the final hole, and then calmly made his putt to defeat Gary Hallberg and Marty West by one stroke.

"I was going for the birdie all the way," explained a happy Cook after his round. "I'm not the best playoff player."

John Cook's arrival in the winners circle was certainly not a fluke. In 1975, at the age of sixteen, the protégé of Ken Venturi won the California Junior, California Amateur, and World Junior titles in one summer. His victory in the 1977 Sunnehanna Amateur was just the beginning of greater success in amateur golf.

John Cook's approach shot on the final hole finished two feet from the hole and led to the winning birdie.

Sunnehanna Amateur

JAY SIGEL

S unnehanna Country Club swung open its doors and members made room in their homes for 58 of the nation's best amateur golfers for the 25th time in 1978. The field, however, was weakened as some college coaches prevented their players from competing in the tournament because of the distance to Johnstown from Eugene, Oregon, the site of the NCAA Championships.

Jay Sigel becomes the third two-time champion.

Defending champion John Cook, as well as Jay Sigel, and Vance Heafner returned to Sunnehanna and the selection process yielded some new and geographically interesting players. Masahiro "Massy" Kuramoto, the two-time Japanese Amateur champion was invited after being recommended by John Cook, who played with him the prior summer. Cook and Ohio State teammate, Mark Balen, looked after Kuramoto during the week, all three staying at the same home.

Kuramoto began the tournament with three consecutive birdies. He then added four birdies and two bogeys over the next fifteen holes to shoot a masterful opening round of 65. The Yokohama golfer was three strokes ahead of Sigel and Heafner as rain interrupted play several times the first day.

On Saturday, three bogeys on the last five holes prevented a runaway by Jay Sigel.

First round leader Massy Kuramoto chips while Jay Sigel looks

In spite of his uncharacteristic finish, Sigel's rounds of 69-69 added to his opening 68 placed him three strokes ahead of another relatively unknown player, Mark Wiebe. Weibe, from Escondido, California, earned his invitation by winning the Idaho Amateur. Three players, Ricky Gregg from the University of Tennessee, Bill Buettner from the University of North Carolina, and Vance Heafner were an additional three strokes behind.

First round leader Kuramoto fell from contention with rounds of 73 and 74, but left a considerable impression on his playing partners. "I'm glad we

Mark Weibe finished second.

aren't playing in Japan," remarked Sigel. "Imagine playing on his turf, eating his food."

Jay Sigel's final margin of victory of two strokes was made closer than it appeared after making three bogeys on his last eight holes.

The final scoreboard mirrored Saturday as Wiebe, who played at San Jose State, recovered from a triple bogey on the second hole to shoot 71 and finish second.

Vance Heafner stood alone in third place in the middle of the fairway on the eighteenth hole, but spectators cringed as he shanked his approach shot into the parking lot. His double bogey tied him with Gregg and Buettner for third place. It was a final frustration for Heafner.

The 1977 North Carolina Amateur and Porter Cup champion, Heafener played spectacular golf from tee-to-green, but a balky putter undermined his fine ball striking. "If Vance had made a few putts today, we would still be playing," the champion commented afterward.

Jay Sigel remained on the grounds of the golf course afterwards, soaking up his victory. The usually stoic Sigel was notably happy after winning his second Sunnehanna Amateur: "I'm very, very, thrilled. The 1976 Sunnehanna was the last real big tourney I won although I did win some others in between."

Vance Heafner finished third in 1978. The North Carolina State All-American was a member of the 1977 US Walker Cup team.

Jay Sigel is followed by a youthful gallery.

Sunnehanna Amateur

JOHN COOK

One of the finest fields in the history of the tournament prepared to compete for the Sunnehanna Amateur title in June of 1979. Jay Sigel could not return, John Cook did. The Amateur was one of the few tournaments that Cook did not win in 1978. The transplanted Californian won the Northeast, Ohio and U.S. Amateurs, finishing the year as the nation's top ranked amateur.

In 1979, John Cook won his second Sunnehanna Amateur title. Cook's other prominent amateur victories included the 1978 and 1979 Northeast Amateur and the 1978 U.S Amateur. Cook has won eleven times on the PGA tour.

The week prior to returning to Johnstown, Cook successfully defended his Northeast Amateur title breaking Ben Crenshaw's tournament record and lapping the field by nine strokes.

Before play began, Cook noted the quality of the field. He expected stiff competition from Bobby Clampett, the California and Western Amateur champion Gary Hallberg, the 1977 and 1978 NCAA champion; Fred Couples, from the University of Houston; and San Jose State's Mark Wiebe, runner-up in the 1978 Sunnehanna Amateur.

The first round was dominated by collegiate players with Cook and Oral Robert's star Joe Rassett leading after opening rounds of 65. Cook appeared on the verge of a course record with a fine score of 31 on the demanding front nine, but cooled off on the final nine holes.

On Saturday, rain again visited Johnstown as play was delayed twice during the day. A long day was made even longer, as players struggled with their games and their concentration. The day ended with John Cook leading Mark Wiebe by a stroke and Fred Couples by two, with Rassett and Clampett an additional stroke behind.

Cook's strategy for the final day was fairly simple. "I just try to shoot birdies and stay under par," explained Cook. "Usually that's all you have to do to win." A member of Ohio State's NCAA championship team, Cook gained control of the tournament early with a birdie from 35 feet on the first hole. On the backside, Cook played flawlessly. Birdies on eleven and twelve essentially insured his second Sunnehanna title as his pursuers staggered around the course.

Wiebe made a pair of double-bogeys on the eighth and eleventh holes and added for good measure bogeys on the fourth, seventh, tenth, sixteenth and eighteenth holes. His day ended mercifully with 77 after a birdie on the first hole, Couples bogeyed the second and third holes. He never got closer than two strokes to the leader.

Gary Hallberg, the NCAA champion, birdied two of the first three holes and then was penalized two strokes on the fourth hole. A short putt struck the back of the cup and then hit the blade of his putter on his follow through, resulting in the penalty.

Runner-up Fred Couples lauded the champion afterward: "I was making the hard pars and he was making easy birdies. I thought it was over when I bogeyed the second and third (holes). I knew it was over when he birdied eleven and twelve."

It was John Cook's final appearance in Johnstown. He announced his intentions to turn professional after losing in the finals of the U.S. Amateur to Mark O'Meara.

The 1979 Sunnehanna Amateur might well have been the strongest in the tournament's history. The field of 65 players included ten players who had been, or would be named, to the United States Walker Cup team, and eleven future champions on the PGA Tour. Four players including Fred Couples, Jeff Sluman, Hal Sutton, and Bob Tway went onto win one of professional golf's four majors titles.

Fred Couples runner-up in 1979.

The final threesome: Couples, Cook and Clampett. Fred Couples was runner-up in the 1979 Sunnehanna Amateur and returned again in 1980. The University of Houston standout has won 15 PGA events including the 1992 Masters.

119

Sunnehanna Amateur

BOBBY CLAMPETT

An unusually large number of amateur qualifiers for the U.S. Open enhanced the quality, if not the quantity, of the field as 54 players vied for the 27th Sunnehanna Amateur title. Among the qualifiers for the Open that was played at Baltusrol the week before the tournament, were Bobby Clampett, Gary Hallberg, Jodie Mudd, Joe Rassett, and Joey Sindelar.

'80

Bobby Clampett shows his winning form. Clampett was a three-time All-American at Brigham Young and was a two-time winner of the Fred Haskins Award, presented to the nation's top collegiate player. Clampett won the 1978 Western Amateur.

Four of the top ten finishers in the recently completed NCAA Championships—Clampett, Rassett, Bob Tway from Oklahoma State, and Fred Couples from the University of Houston—also entered the tournament.

High winds and cold temperatures punished the players the first day as a cold front dropped temperatures to 35-degrees overnight. Winds blew at 30-mph, with gusts that exceeded 50-mph, and resulted in the highest first round scores ever.

The first round leader was Curt Byrum whose opening round of 69 was the only score below par. A testament to the difficult opening-round conditions was apparent with one look at the scoreboard. Twenty-four players in a field of 54 shot 79 or higher, making for the worst first day scores in the tournament's history.

Curt Byrum, first round leader.

The next day perfect conditions existed and Bobby Clampett took control of the tournament. A morning round of 70 tied him for the 36-hole lead with David Ogrin of Texas A&M. An afternoon round of 66, put him four strokes ahead of Wake Forest's Gary Hallberg. The field essentially conceded the tournament to Clampett who battled good friend John Cook

Bob Tway was a three-time first team All-American at Oklahoma State. In 1986, he was PGA Player of the Year.

for the nation's top amateur ranking in 1979.

"All we can do is go out and play as well as we can," said first-round leader Curt Byrum who was in third place five strokes behind.

On the final day, spectators witnessed a wobbly Bobby Clampett struggle to maintain his lead. The leader shot 2-over-par on the front nine while Gary Hallberg shot 1-under par to cut Clampett's lead to a single stroke.

"I knew finishing up the front nine that Gary was one back. I told myself I better get going. I know what kind of golfer he is because we've had battles in the past." Clampett said afterwards.

But Hallberg's thoughts of winning his final amateur tournament disappeared on the usually easy eleventh hole with one swing. There his drive missed the fairway and came to rest among the pine trees on the right. From there he struggled to make a bogey.

Gary Hallberg finished runner-up for the second time at Sunnehanna in 1981. He was the first four-time first team All-American in NCAA golf history.

While his playing partner struggled, Clampett split the fairway on the same hole with his drive and his second shot with a 3-wood finished ten feet from the pin. It was the best shot of the tournament. Clampett's eagle putt found the bottom of the cup and essentially ended the tournament.

For runner-up Gary Hallberg, the first four-time first team All-American in the history of NCAA golf, it was a bittersweet way to end his amateur career. Hallberg, who also finished runner-up in the 1977 Sunnehanna Amateur, turned his attention to professional golf. His first planned professional start was the Western Open. His goal for the year was to make the $8,000, required to automatically give him playing privileges on the PGA tour and avoid the dreaded Q-school.

After signing his scorecard and accepting the winner's trophy, Clampett's thoughts turned to a flight back to California.

He had an 8:30 tee time the next day in the California Amateur, but Clampett knew the long flight back would be a little easier having won the Sunnehanna Amateur: "This is the finest amateur tournament in the country. The win means a lot to me."

After another successful summer, Bobby Clampett, like his good friend John Cook, decided to forego his senior year at Brigham Young and turn professional.

Sunnehanna Amateur

JODIE MUDD

*I*n spite of losing several prominent players to the professional ranks, the 1981 Sunnehanna Amateur had a record field of 74 players. The top returning players from the 1980 Sunnehanna Amateur were third-place finishers Curt Byrum and Jodie Mudd, an All-American golfer from Georgia Southern.

Other top collegiate players coming to Johnstown included Willie Wood from Oklahoma State, Steve Jones from Colorado, Keith Clearwater from Bringham Young, and late addition Ron Commans from USC. Commans won five collegiate tournaments in 1981 and added the NCAA individual title to cap off a great year.

Six of eight first team NCAA All-Americans also accepted invitations to play.

Hal Sutton, one year removed from the collegiate ranks, was considered by many to be the player to beat. The nation's top-ranked amateur, Sutton was the reigning U.S. Amateur champion, had won two Western Amateur titles, the North and South Amateur, and the Northeast Amateur. He arrived at Sunnehanna in a bit of a slump having recently missed the cut in several PGA events.

Jodie Mudd turned professional in 1982 and won four times. In 1990, Mudd captured the Players Championship and the Tour Championship.

Hal Sutton walks off the first tee with Todd Thiele. In 1980, Sutton won his second Western Amateur, the Northeast Amateur and the US Amateur. He has won 14 times on the PGA Tour including the 1983 PGA Championship.

Play began with perfect conditions for a change and at the day's end Jodie Mudd was at the top of the leader board after an opening round of 67. Mudd's first round was an extension of his fine play in 1980 when he finished with rounds of 69-69-67 after an opening round of 80.

On Saturday, Mudd struggled following an opening nine of 35. He opened the back nine on the first hole with a bogey and then added four consecutive bogeys on holes five through eight and shot 39. Steve Jones, Willie Wood, and

Sunnehanna Amateur

Canadian Amateur Champion Greg Olson took the 36-hole lead at 136.

In the afternoon, Mudd recovered, firing a scintillating front nine of 31 highlighted by a holed wedge for eagle three on the ninth hole. Only a single bogey on the thirteenth hole prevented Mudd from tying the course record. His afternoon round of 64 put him back in the lead.

"I knew I was going to need at least 67 to get back," Mudd said. "I knew with that, I would be right around the lead."

Two strokes behind were Steve Jones, Willie Wood, and Ohio State All-American, Joey Sindelar. As for Sutton, his slump continued as rounds of 75-78-74 put him on the lower half of the scoreboard.

On Sunday, Jodie Mudd struggled. The eighth hole claimed another leader, as Mudd's drive rattled among the trees on the right. When his ball was found Mudd declared his ball unplayable, invoked Rule 28-a and returned to the tee. Only a missed five-foot birdie putt by Clearwater prevented the damage from being worse for Mudd, who made a double-bogey six.

"I don't know what happened," said Mudd. "I hadn't had any problems with that hole all week. I must have rushed it a bit and hit it thin."

At the turn Mudd maintained a tenuous one-shot lead over Wood and Clearwater. On the backside, however, Mudd regained his composure, and the lead, going into the final hole. Wood and Clearwater were a stroke behind having missed numerous opportunities to take the lead.

There were no eighteenth hole heroics as Wood missed the green and settled for a par and a final round of 69. Clearwater badly missed his putt for birdie and his final round of 68 fell one stroke short of catching Mudd.

Jodie Mudd, a product of municipal golf and the reigning U.S. Public Links champion, grew up on the other side of the tracks from most of his fellow competitors.

"I've always felt like I was underprivileged as far as golf was concerned," he said afterwards. "It helped me along the way. It gave me more drive."

Mudd permitted himself a large smile contemplating his drive home to Louisville and to the municipal course he still called home. The champion of the Sunnehanna Amateur, Mudd was justifiably proud of his victory, "I wanted this one [the Sunnehanna Amateur] badly ever since last year. I'm very comfortable here. This is a great tournament, run by great people. Winning here means a lot to me and I just love this course."

Steve Jones finished sixth in the 1981 Sunnehanna Amateur. The University of Colorado standout has eight PGA victories to his credit. In 1996, Jones won the US Open at Oakland Hills, defeating Davis Love and Tom Lehman by one stroke.

Sunnehanna Amateur

BRAD FAXON

A modest field of 54 players were welcomed to Sunnehanna in June of 1982. Keith Clearwater, runner-up in the 1981 Sunnehanna Amateur, and Jay Sigel, who won his second Porter Cup title in 1981, were the early favorites.

Other players receiving early attention were Brad Faxon, who finished third place in the prior week's NCAA Championship and recently quali-

fied for the U.S. Open, and Frank Fuhrer from Pittsburgh who played at the University of North Carolina. Fuhrer was the nation's second-ranked amateur and the 1981 Western Amateur champion.

The player's slogged around a waterlogged course and after the first day, Roy Biancalana of LSU led with a score of 67. Only two other players, Brad Faxon with 68 and Jim Carter with 69, managed to break par. Other notable names near the top of the scoreboard included Tom Lehman with 70, and defending U.S. Mid-Amateur champion Jim Holtgrieve, as well as Davis Love and Frank Fuhrer.

Brad Faxon defeated Tom Lehman and Jay Sigel by two strokes to win the title. In 1983, Faxon was a member of the Walker Cup team and won the Fred Haskins Award. He turned professional the same year and has won seven times on tour.

Frank Fuhrer from Pittsburgh was one of the nation's best amateurs.

Steady rains again greeted the players on Saturday and at the end of the day Tom Lehman, the Minnesota Stroke and Match Play champion, led Brad Faxon and Jay Sigel by two strokes.

On Sunday, Lehman battled the elements, and his game, so much so that by the sixth tee, Jay Sigel had tied Lehman. Brad Faxon trailed the leaders by four strokes after making bogeys on two of his first three holes, but fought back making birdies on the sixth, seventh, and ninth holes. While Faxon rallied, Lehman added bogeys on six and eight to fall behind the leader. Sigel staggered home finishing the front nine with consecutive bogeys on the final two holes.

With the momentum clearly tilted in his direction, it was Brad Faxon's tournament to win. The leader continued his solid play on the backside narrowly missing birdie putts to extend his lead. Tom Lehman rallied, and by the time Faxon reached the 189-yard par three fourteenth hole, Lehman had methodically closed his lead to a single stroke. Jay Sigel had also closed the gap with Faxon trailing the leader by two strokes.

On the par 3, Faxon removed his nemesis from his bag: a long iron. Faxon let it rip. His shot finished 20 feet away from the cup.

"I decided I had to go with the one iron anyway," Faxon said. "Sure I was talking to myself. I said, 'Keep a good tempo and kill it!'"

After Lehman and Sigel missed their birdie putts, Faxon's putter came through and widened his lead to two strokes with four holes to play. Four pars later, Brad Faxon captured his first major amateur title, defeating Jay Sigel and Tom Lehman by two strokes.

"I was a little bit confident with that lead after 14," the winner later said. "But then, Tom was hitting all the greens, so I couldn't get too confident."

Prior to winning the Sunnehanna Amateur, Faxon's biggest win had been the New England Amateur.

"This is a big win for sure," said Faxon, "The goal of every amateur is to play on the Walker Cup team and things like that. You have to win tournaments like this to make that step."

Tom Lehman, was runner-up with Jay Sigel in 1983. Lehman led the tournament after 54-holes but a final round of 73 opened the door for Brad Faxon. Lehman's professional career includes five victories, including the 1996 British Open.

Faxon's reputation with the putter was well deserved and apparent to the brave souls who ventured onto the course to watch the final round. The champion made 120 feet worth of putts. His four birdies on holes six, eight, nine and fourteen came from 30, 50, 10, and 30 feet respectively, and this didn't even count the innumerable putts from similar distances that grazed the whole.

"I thought Brad played excellent... I never saw a guy putt like that," said a somewhat jealous Lehman afterward.

Brad Faxon studies a put.

Sunnehanna Amateur

DILLARD PRUITT

Dillard Pruitt

New faces were prevalent around the grounds of Sunnehanna Country Club before play began in 1983. Among the 61 contestants included first-time competitors such as Oklahoma State's Scott Verplank, the Texas Amateur champion and the nation's second-ranked junior in 1982. Billy Ray Brown, the 1982 NCAA champion from Houston, and Chris Perry, the 1982 Northeast Amateur champion from Ohio State, entered the tournament for the first time.

Marty West, a two-time member of the Walker Cup team, was runner-up in the Sunnehanna Amateur four times.

Two-time Sunnehanna Amateur champion, Jay Sigel, returned as the nation's top-ranked amateur. Fellow Mid-Am's, Marty West, a six-time Maryland Amateur champion; Jim Holtgrieve, fifth at Sunnehanna in 1982; and Bob Lewis, runner-up in the 1981 U.S. Amateur were all considered legitimate contenders for the title. All hoped to end the stranglehold that college players had on the tournament title.

Low scores were abundant the first day, particularly on the backside as eighteen players broke par, and another nine players shot even-par on the inward nine. Jim Holtgrieve, the former U.S. Mid-Amateur champion, took the lead with an opening round of 65. Another stroke back was University of Houston star and NCAA champion, Billy Ray Brown who shot 66 in spite of a viral infection contracted the day before.

After Saturday's double round, Marty West, the popular veteran from Rockville, Maryland, was in the lead. Two shots behind was John Slaughter, the nation's fifth-ranked amateur, and All-American John Inman who was also the Atlantic Coast Conference and Eastern Amateur champion. Billy Andrade, a sophomore at Wake Forest, was two shots behind.

Sunnehanna Amateur

Jim Holtgrieve is helped by his caddie Dave Bernardi. Holtgrieve finished third in 1983.

West was playing in his eleventh Sunnehanna Amateur. This was his best opportunity to capture the title that he had coveted after his first appearance in 1972. Twice a member of the Walker Cup team, he finished tied for second in the Sunnehanna Amateur three times before: in 1972, 1974 and 1977.

The tournament was decided on one hole, the fairly benign par 3 sixteenth hole. West, three holes from capturing the title and two strokes ahead, missed the green badly to the right. His subsequent pitch rolled the length of the fast, slopping green, finishing on the fringe some 50 feet from the pin. Three putts later his lead was gone. West's playing partner, Billy Andrade, faired even worse on the same hole making a triple-bogey six that eliminated him from competition.

After another bogey on seventeen by West, and Clemson University golfer, Dillard Pruitt, was suddenly in the lead.

"I couldn't believe when I heard what happened down at 16," Pruitt said afterward.

Deflated by his play on the previous holes, West could not muster the birdie needed to force a playoff. Dillard Pruitt, the 1982 South Carolina Amateur champion, won the Sunnehanna Amateur title.

The newly crowned champion's final round score of 68 was one of only two sub-par rounds that day; the other was by Jay Sigel. He also birdied four of Sunnehanna's five par 3's avoiding the pratfalls that befelled West and Andrade.

"When I came off 18," recalled a stunned Pruitt, "someone told me Billy tripled and Marty doubled. I said to myself, 'Maybe I can win this thing.'"

A dejected West contemplates what might have been.

Sunnehanna Amateur

SCOTT VERPLANK

The 62 participants in the 1984 Sunnehanna Amateur included four of the top five finishers from 1983, among them defending champion Dillard Pruitt, Scott Verplank and newcomers such as Steve Elkington.

The field was one of the deepest in the history of the tournament. Among the top ranked amateurs were Verplank, the 1983 Porter Cup champion from Oklahoma State; Brandel Chamblee, the 1983 Rice Planters champion from the University of Texas, Dillard Pruitt; Steve Elkington, the Southwest Conference champion from Houston; and Bill Hadden, the 1983 Northeast Amateur champion.

Two players from the University of North Carolina, John Inman, the recently crowned NCAA champion and Davis Love, the 1984 North and South and Atlantic Coast Conference champion, added depth and ability to the tournament field.

Scott Verplank won back-to-back Sunnehanna Amateur titles in 1984 and 1985. Later in 1984, Verplank added the Western Amateur, Texas Amateur and U.S. Amateur titles. His amateur career included the NCAA and Porter Cup titles. In 1985, Verplank became the first amateur since Gene Littler to win a PGA event. As a professional, Verplank has won three times.

Friday found John Inman and Steve Elkington leading after the first day with rounds of 67. Elkington, a native of Wollongong, Australia, was unaware of the Sunnehanna Amateur until teammate Billy Ray Brown told him about it. A single shot back were Clark Burroughs and Scott Verplank, whose round highlighted by chip-in birdies on both the ninth and eighteenth holes.

Possibly the longest day in amateur golf was made longer after 40-minute rain delay but Scott Verplank seemed unfazed. While first round leader Inman struggled during the morning round, Verplank seized control of the tournament following his first round of 68 with a fine morning round of 65. Elkington was his closest pursuer shooting 68.

Fatigue was a common refrain among competitors at the close of Saturdays play. Verplank wobbled at times on his closing nine holes, a possible result of his struggle with diabetes, making bogeys on eleven, a result of an unplayable lie, thirteen and seventeen, but those miscues were offset by birdies on ten, fifteen and sixteen. With one round to play the Dallas, Texas native lead Elkington by three-strokes. John Inman, who recovered with an afternoon

Sunnehanna Amateur

Steve Elkington finished third in the 1984 Sunnehanna Amateur. The University of Houston All-American joined the PGA Tour in 1987 and has won 10 times. In 1995, he won the PGA Championship.

round of 68, David Tolley and Bill Hadden were five strokes back behind the leader.

On the final day, spectators witnessed a fast start by Verplank with birdies on the first and third holes and most assumed the tournament was over. Then the unexpected happened as the Oklahoma State junior-to-be made three straight bogeys on the sixth, seventh and eigth holes and finished the front nine at one over par 36.

While Verplank fought to regain his control of his game David Tolley briefly closed the gap too two strokes with a birdie on the thirteenth hole. Not to be outdone, Verplank matched Tolleys birdie. His approach shot on the same hole finished four feet from the pin to widen his lead back to three strokes. "I had a pretty good lead after five holes and I thought I was going to blow the course down," said Verplank,"but after I made those bogeys I was just trying to make par but that birdie on 13 helped."

On the fifteenth hole, Verplank's comfortable lead again seemed to be in doubt when his drive on the par five ended up under trees. Taking a few practice swings before playing his next shot, spectators asserted that he had broken branches in the process. Discussions ensued and tournament czar Bill Price and Paul Petrovich ruled that no infraction occurred. Play resumed with no penalty strokes assessed and Verplank made a fine par.

David Tolley battled on finishing his round with consecutive birdies on the final two holes. His back nine round of 31 and final round of 66 fell a single shot short of catching Scott Verplank. That single shot could be found during Saturdays play. A holed chip shot by Tolley on the twelfth hole was nullified when his caddy yanked the pin from the hole, the ball returned to the surface of the green and his birdie became a tap-in par.

In 1985 Scott Verplank returned as the nation's top ranked amateur. After capturing the Sunnehanna Amateur in 1984, he won his second Texas Amateur, the Western Amateur and ended the summer defeating Sam Randolph to win the US Amateur.

The two-time, first-team All-American returned to Sunnehanna after competing in the Northeast Amateur where he was defeated by Jay Sigel by two strokes. By his own admission, Verplank's game was not what it was the prior year although he felt energized by his recent play. The attention and self-imposed pressure took its toll on the tightly wound Verplank. The defending champion's chief antagonist was expected to be Jay Sigel.

From the collegiate ranks, competition was expected to come from Davis Love, the nations fourth ranked amateur from North Carolina. Love

Sunnehanna Amateur

won three titles in 1984, the Atlantic Coast Conference, the North-South Amateur and the Middle-Atlantic Amateur. University of Florida golfer Scott Dunlap, the 1984 Southern Amateur champion was the nations sixth ranked amateur, and Clark Burroughs from Ohio State, the 1985 Big Ten and NCAA individual champion, were expected to contend for the title.

Davis Love's best finish was tied for fourth in 1985. Love turned professional in the fall of 1985 and has won 19 tour titles including the 1997 PGA at Winged Foot.

To know ones surprise, the Oklahoma State Cowboy shot an inspired opening round of 66 to take a one shot lead over Pittsburgh native Bob Friend and Jim Holtgrieve. A front nine of 32, on the normally difficult outward nine was not extraordinary as players took advantage of near perfect conditions. Seventeen players in the field of 64 players shot par or better the first day, the best opening scores in events history.

Round two was more of the same as Verplank continued to batter the course and the field adding 67 to his stanza. Just as he did the prior year, the defending champion struggled at times in the afternoon and finished his round with a double-bogey on his final hole of the day. The defending champion was still in the lead by two strokes over Scott Dunlap and Jim Holtgrieve.

There was no repeat of the prior year's final round escapades, playing in front of the largest crowds in the history of the tournament, Verplank sprinted around the front nine with birdies on the second, fourth, and ninth holes, his only blemish a bogey on the third hole. After birdies on the tenth and eleventh holes, Verplank's thoughts turned to Bobby Greenwood's tournament record but a bogey on the fourteenth hole and pars on the remaining four holes left him a shot short of the record.

His final round of 66 defeated Jay Sigel by a tournament record seven strokes with Jim Holtgrieve finishing in third eight strokes behind. "There is nothing frustrating about watching a good 66," commented Holtgrieve. "In fact that's fun to watch."

"It feels great now that it's over," said Verplank who maintained his usual intensity in spite of the large lead. "I wasn't worried like I was last year." With his victory Scott Verplank became the first Sunnehanna Amateur champion to successfully defend his title. Several weeks later the two-time Sunnehanna Amateur champion won the Western Open adding to his considerable reputation by becoming the first amateur since Gene Littler in 1954 to win a PGA tour event as an amateur.

Sunnehanna Amateur

BILLY ANDRADE

Billy Andrade turned professional in 1987 and has won four times on tour.

The week prior to play, two-time Sunnehanna Amateur champion Scott Verplank added the NCAA Individual title to his trophy case. Thankfully for the Sunnehanna Amateur's 72 contestants, it was his final amateur title and event.

'86

The 1986 tournament field included 1985 runner-up Jay Sigel, third place finisher Jim Holtgrieve, and two players who finished tied for fourth: Greg Parker and Bob Friend. Friend came to the tournament on a hot streak. The son of the former Pittsburgh Pirate pitcher, Friend had won the Monroe Invitational and Northeast Amateur back-to-back.

Bob Friend came to Johnstown as a pre-tournament favorite in 1986. A recent graduate of LSU, the Pittsburgh native finished fourth at Sunnehanna in 1985.

Billy Andrade and Len Mattiace, members of Wake Forest's 1986 NCAA Championship team, also returned to Johnstown. Andrade won the 1986 North-South Amateur and was ranked tenth nationally among amateur golfers. Mattiace, won the 1985 Southern Amateur and was ranked eighth among amateur golfers.

First-time competitors added quality to the field as Arizona State's Billy Mayfair and Texas Christian's Jim Sorenson, the 1985 U. S. Public Links Champion from Texas Christian, accepted invitations. After the conclusion of the first round, Greg Parker from the University of North Carolina led Sorenson and Andrade. His first-round score of 65 placed him two and three shots ahead of each respectively.

After Saturday's play, Billy Andrade and Mike Podolak were tied at three under-par 207. Andrade was aided by a birdie-eagle finish on his final two holes of the day. One shot behind was Parker and two strokes behind was Sorenson.

Sunnehanna Amateur

The tournament was decided on three holes. Arriving at the eleventh tee, Podolak and Sorenson were two-under par and one ahead of Andrade and Parker, who were playing in the group behind them. A pulled second shot on the eleventh by Sorenson finished in the trees and led to a disastrous bogey on the course's easiest hole.

Andrade took advantage of the same hole, his second shot finishing ten feet from the cup on the par-5. After making his eagle putt, he proceeded to birdie the twelfth hole and take a two-stroke lead.

" I'd been hanging around the lead all day, but I had to do something if I was going to win," said Andrade. "If I didn't make a move I had no chance."

On the thirteenth hole, Andrade's wedge from 105 yards out found its way into the cup. By day's end Billy Andrade had defeated Jim Sorenson by four strokes and Len Mattiace, who rallied the final day with a 66, by six strokes.

Len Mattiace finished in third six strokes behind Wake Forest teammate Billy Andrade in 1986.

Billy Andrade's eagle-birdie-eagle tirade won him the tournament. It also obliterated the painful memories of 1993 when a triple-bogey six on the sixteenth hole ended his chance of winning the tournament.

"That came back to me as soon as I got to the tee," remembered Andrade. "Four years ago I'd blown it, but four years have made a lot of difference."

Bill Andrade and Jim Sorenson reach the eighteenth green. Joe Shorto Sunnehanna Professional was marker for the final group.

Sunnehanna Amateur

GREG LESHER

The concurrent playing of the Northeast Amateur weakened the field the 34th Sunnehanna Amateur title. The most prominent college players returning to Sunnehanna were first team All-Americans Bob Estes from the University of Texas and Greg Parker from North Carolina, as well as second team All-American Rob McNamara from LSU.

'87

Greg Lesher

Middle amateurs, players over 25-years of age, hoped to break the collegiate stranglehold on the tournament title. Reinstated amateurs Mike Podolak, the 1984 U.S. Mid-Amateur champion, and Bill Loeffler, who won the same title in 1986, were the likeliest contenders.

A tournament that seemed to assure firsts did just that as 57-year-old Bo Williams, the reigning U.S. Senior Amateur champion, shot 67 and finished the day tied with Rob McNamara. It was, and is today, the only time a senior golfer has been atop the leader board at the close of a day's play. A shot behind the leaders was Lebanon, Pennsylvania native and LSU golfer, Greg Lesher.

On Saturday, Rob McNamara took advantage of miserable conditions to pull away from the field. After the morning round, the Southern Amateur champion, who defended his title later that summer, stood at four under par, three shots ahead of Marty West and Joe Malay.

Malay received considerable atten-

Rob McNamara, three-time LSU All-American and two-time Southern Amateur champion.

Skip Kendall

Spectators respond to Lesher's bunker shot on sixteen.

tion for his invention of a pressurized driver. A valve stem protruding from the grip permitted air to be pumped into the shaft before play. Just when you think you have seen it all!

After the third round, McNamara left the course four strokes ahead of Marty West and five strokes ahead of Lesher and UNLV's Skip Kendall. His lead, however, could have been bigger: A birdie-eagle-birdie streak on holes three through five were thrown away by bogeys on six and seven and a double-bogey on nine.

The final day was a story of the student defeating the teacher. Greg Lesher came back to defeat his teammate by shooting a bogey-free round of 65 highlighted by a holed bunker shot on sixteen for birdie.

McNamara took Lesher under his wing during his freshman year, trying to provide encouragement to his teammate who struggled with his confidence. As the gregarious McNamara stated afterwards, "We can clearly say the boy is over that, can't we."

Lesher tipped his cap to his mentor afterwards, "It was pretty gratifying today, beating Rob because without him, there's no way I'd have been able to take the winner's bowl today,"

The one-two finish by the LSU tandem was the first time players from the same college team finished atop the Sunnehanna scoreboard.

Marty West and Rob McNamara watch as Greg Lesher tees-off on seventeen.

Sunnehanna Amateur
JAY SIGEL

Fifty-six of the nation's top players met again in 1988 hoping to capture one of amateur golf's most prestigious titles. Joining returning champion Greg Lesher were four of the nation's top ten players. Among them Jay Sigel, who won his third U.S. Mid-Amateur as well as the Porter Cup in 1987, Bob Lewis the 1987 Northeast Amateur champion, Billy Mayfair, and Kevin Johnson.

Kevin Johnson was the nation's fourth-ranked amateur. In 1987, Johnson, who played at Clemson won the U.S. Public Links title and the Massachusetts Amateur. Billy Mayfair, the 1987 U.S. Amateur champion and the 1986 U.S. Public Links champion from Arizona State, was named winner of the Fred Haskins Award given annually to the nation's best collegiate player.

Jay Sigel becomes the tournament's first three-time champion.

When the first day was completed, players, usually inclined to discuss their rounds, turned their wrath on the first day's pin placements. Complaints were heard from players of all ages and backgrounds. First-round leader Robert Gamez charitably called them a "joke." Jay Sigel was even harsher in his assessment of the course setup. Even mild-mannered Roger McManus, playing in his 28th Sunnehanna Amateur, voiced his displeasure.

The pin placements and gusty winds reeked havoc with the field as Gamez, a resident of Las Vegas, opened with 68; he was the only player to break par. Firs round scores were comparable with those in 1980 as nineteen of the 56 players shot 79 or higher.

Unseasonably high winds continued for a second day and scoring remained difficult. Gamez still led after the second round in spite of shooting a 73. In the afternoon scores ballooned, and by the day's end, Tim Dunlavey from Erie, Pennsylvania and the University of Virginia led Petey King and Jay Sigel by two strokes. Dunlavey's total of three over par 213 was the first time

Robert Gamez tied for second.

the leader's three-round, 54 hole total was above par.

On the final day, high winds continued to challenge the players. Jay Sigel's experience and course knowledge proved invaluable. Eschewing his driver for a 3-wood or 2-iron, Sigel succeeded where his competition failed: keeping his ball in the fairway off the tee. Sigel's final round 68 defeated Robert Gamez and Mike Podolak by five shots.

His first round criticism long forgotten, the first three-time champion praised the course and Mark Hollick, the course superintendent and the man responsible for the pin placements.

"I'm simply awed by this course," Sigel gushed afterwards, "This is the best (condition) I've seen this course in 19 years."

Jay Sigel's third victory came ten years after his second victory and ended the nine-year stranglehold on the Sunnehanna Amateur title by college players.

"It's tough enough to win once here, and a second win is even nicer," remarked Sigel. "But a third win, especially since this was one of the best fields ever here, that's something special."

The nation's top collegiate player in 1988, Billy Mayfair, won the U.S. Amateur in 1986 and the U.S. Public Links title in 1987.

Sunnehanna Amateur

ALLEN DOYLE

A series of late cancellations cut the field to 57 players as previous champions Jay Sigel, who had played in 20 consecutive tournaments, and Greg Lesher withdrew from the tournament. Both had qualified for the U. S. Open, which coincided with the playing Sunnehanna Amateur.

Allen Doyle wins his first title.

Robert Gamez, 1988 runner-up at Sunnehanna and runner-up in the 1989 NCAA Championship, did return. The prior summer he reached the quarter-finals in the U.S. Amateur and U.S. Public Links.

Other collegiate All-Americans in the field were University of Oklahoma's Doug Martin, and Len Mattiace from Wake Forest. Martin finished fourth at Sunnehanna in 1988, and later that summer reached the semi-finals of the 1988 U.S. Amateur. Mattiace won the 1989 Dixie Amateur.

Allen Doyle

Mid-Amateurs considered the likeliest candidates to fill Jay Sigel's large shoes were Ralph Howe, the 1988 U.S. Public Links and Middle Atlantic Amateur champion, and Allen Doyle. Doyle was making his third appearance in Johnstown after a three-year absence. In 1988, he won his fifth Georgia Amateur and third Southeastern Amateur title.

At the conclusion of the first day's play, Sean Gorgone from Miami of Ohio sat atop of the leader board with a score of 67. Gorgone, the two-time Maine Amateur champion from Topsham, Maine, led Doug Martin and Steve Frisch by one stroke.

On Saturday, bright sunshine and light winds appeared and so did luck, and lots of it, for Allen Doyle. After a morning round of

68, Doyle eagled two of his final seven holes to shoot his second 68 of the day. In the afternoon, Doyle reached his eleventh hole (Sunnehanna's third hole) two over par until his second shot with a 9-iron on the par 4 found the bottom of the cup. Even par for his round, Doyle scrambled on both the fifth and sixth holes saving par from greenside bunkers. Still even par for his round on the par 5 ninth, his final hole of the day, Doyle again pulled out his trusty 9-iron. He watched in amazement as his ball again disappeared into the hole. His 207-total put him four strokes ahead of Jason Widener, the 1988 U.S. Junior champion and the nation's top ranked junior. Five strokes

Steve Stricker

behind Doyle was Doug Martin and University of Illinois All-American Steve Stricker.

Watching the leader prepare for the final round one onlooker said, "If you saw this guy warming up on the driving range, you'd be wondering how much you could take from him on the course."

Doyle answered comments like that with solid golf. Widener, within a stroke of Doyle made a double-bogey after hitting his 4-wood into the trees on the right.

Doyle exhibited steady, mistake-free golf over the final four holes to win the 1989 Sunnehanna Amateur defeating Jason Widener by a single stroke. It was Allen Doyle's first major amateur championship. Steve Stricker, the two-time Big Ten champion finished third, two-strokes behind.

"It was just another consistent round," Doyle said. "I felt the key would be to keep the ball in play and it was. I hit 17 greens and didn't make any mistakes."

Jason Widener finished second

Sunnehanna Amateur

Allen Doyle returned to defend his title in 1990, and after a one-year absence, so did Jay Sigel. Jason Widener, runner-up in the 1989 Sunnehanna Amateur and the 1989 Southern Amateur champion, also returned. He had just completed his freshman year at Duke University.

The most notable first-time entrants were All-Americans Kevin Wentworth from Oklahoma State, David Duval from Georgia Tech, and Phil Mickelson from Arizona State. Wentworth, a left-hander, finished runner-up in the 1989 NCAA Championships and won his second-straight Big Eight title in 1990. He also was named first team All-American for the third straight year.

In 1990, Jay Sigel finished runner-up a third time.

Duval, the 1989 U.S. Junior champion, was a first team All-American his freshman year at Georgia Tech. Mickelson, a member of the 1989 Walker Cup team was the nation's second-ranked amateur in 1989. He had also won back-to-back NCAA championships.

When play began, Allen Doyle continued his trademark steady play from tee-to-green leading after the first and second rounds with a two-round total five under-par 135. Three stroke behind were John Harris from Edina, Minnesota and Mike Goodes from Reedsville, North Carolina.

The third round was suspended due to severe thunderstorms as lightning struck the course numerous times. One lightning bolt hit a pine tree close to the first tee setting it ablaze. When play resumed, the Grounds Crew was still extinguishing the fire. A second severe storm permanently ended play for the day.

Two champions: Jay Sigel and Allen Doyle

Prior to the beginning of the tournament, one of the All-American entrants expected intense competition for the title. He specifically noted the presence of the best collegiate players in the country. When asked about the veteran amateurs like Jay Sigel and Allen Doyle he replied, "Oh, they're old. They can't keep up with us young guys."

After the third round

of golf was completed on Sunday, Allen Doyle had lengthened his lead to five strokes over John Harris, the three-time Minnesota Stroke Play champion, and six-strokes over Jay Sigel.

If there was any doubt as to the outcome of the tournament, Allen Doyle quickly put that notion to rest with birdies on the first and third holes. With fifteen holes to play and an eight-stroke lead over Sigel, Doyle elected to play conservative golf. It was a decision that almost came back to haunt him.

"I may have made a mistake in getting conservative a little to early," Doyle later commented. "Once I birdied three, I got real defensive and didn't hit the ball well."

Jay Sigel, six strokes behind and with nothing to lose, made a final push to catch the leader. After a birdie on eleven, Sigel narrowly missed birdies on twelve and thirteen. He then made birdies on fourteen, fifteen, seven, and eighteen to close Doyle's final margin of victory to two strokes.

Afterward, Franklin Langham, the third-place finisher from the University of Georgia and a native of Thomson, Georgia commented, "It's just like home. Everyone else ends up playing for second while Mr. Doyle cleans up." Referring to Doyle's domination of Georgia amateur golf, he added, "He won't give you much. You have to go get him and that's not easy."

Phil Mickelson tees-off

Sunnehanna Amateur
PAUL CLAXTON

*T*he pre-tournament buzz was about the return of Allen Doyle, Jay Sigel, and David Duval. All three were early selections to the 1991 Walker Cup team.

Allen Doyle was attempting to win his third straight Sunnehanna Amateur. In 1990, the two-time defending champion won the Rice Planters (second time), Southeastern Amateur (fourth time), and Georgia Amateur (sixth time).

Jay Sigel arrived in Johnstown having just won his third Northeast Amateur title. David Duval, runner-up in the NCAA Championships, was best remembered for bending his putter in anger during the previous year's opening round. He finished his round putting with his 3-wood.

Paul Claxton

After the first round, the early favorites were over par and unhappy. The player's ire was directed at a course setup that featured wet landing areas, wet fringes, and dried out greens.

"I know everyone had to play the same course, but when you hit a good drive you ought to be rewarded," said Doyle. He spoke for many players when he also said:. "When you water the landing areas with your tees so far back, that's not particularly fair."

Sunnehanna Professional Joe Shorto defended the set-up the best he could to Doyle and the players who surrounded him, asking "What about last year, when it rained the whole time?" Jay Sigel, who angered some Sunnehanna members with his comments, quickly retorted, "What's that have to do with it? It didn't rain today!"

After the completion of the morning eighteen on Saturday, Paul Claxton, the 1990 Cardinal Amateur champion, led the tournament. Bob Lewis and Ron Wuensche were two strokes behind followed by Justin Leonard and Craig Hainline. The real winner after three rounds of play was the golf course. No player broke par for three rounds; Claxton was even par for the three rounds.

The tournament was again decided, as it had been so many times before, on the eighth hole. Still two strokes away, Claxton cut his tee shot. A ball flight that usually ended tragically, all listed as the ball rattled among the trees. Claxton and his fellow competitors watched in stunned disbelief as the ball was jettisoned from disaster into the middle of the fairway.

"Unbelievable," said Lewis who was paired with Claxton the final day.

Taking advantage of his good fortune, Claxton pitched his ball to eight feet, then drained his birdie putt. Claxton's birdie essentially ended his pursuer's hopes of catching him as birdies remained elusive.

"I was very fortunate," said Claxton. "But to say I won the tournament because of that would be short-sighted."

Claxton's final round of 67 was eclipsed only by David Duval who shot 66 on Sunday, the low round of the week. He defeated runner-up Bob Lewis by six strokes and third place finisher Duval by nine strokes The two-time All-American from Vidalia, Georgia and the University of Georgia was the only player to break par for the tournament.

Bob Lewis runner-up in 1991. Lewis was captan of the Walker Cup team in 2003.

David Duval's final round of 66 catapulted him into third place.

Sunnehanna Amateur

ALLEN DOYLE

Paul Claxton, Justin Leonard, and Allen Doyle returned to Sunnehanna hoping to capture the title in 1992, but a 16-year-old from California received most of the early attention.

'92

The arrival of Tiger Woods, who just completed his sophomore year in high school, was widely anticipated. Earlier that year, he became the youngest player to play in a PGA event, competing in the Los Angeles Open. The prior summer, Woods won the U.S.

Allen Doyle wins his third title.

Junior and World Junior titles. Accompanied by his father Earl, the young phenom had been attracting headlines for most of his young life. He was just beginning his rise to the top of amateur golf.

For a change, the players were greeted by perfect conditions. Tied for the lead after opening rounds of 69 on the first day's play was defending champion Paul Claxton, as well as Allen Doyle, Tiger Woods, and John Harris.

At the end of Saturday's double round, Allen Doyle was well on his way to capturing his third Sunnehanna Amateur title. Nine strokes ahead of his closest competitor, Doyle put on a masterful display of golf over the firm Sunnehanna golf course. His morning round of 66 was followed by an afternoon round of 65.

Paired with Wake Forest's Hans Albertson and Woods, Doyle took advantage of the fast course, which set up perfectly for his low-ball flight. The Georgia golfer played bump-and-run golf that would have made course architect A. W. Tillinghast's eyes twinkle with delight. It was golf fit for a museum, and something for any spectator to remember.

Nine strokes behind the leader was Scott Peterson, the two-time Colorado Amateur and the Southwestern Amateur champion. Peterson made

Tiger Woods, age 16

Sunnehanna Amateur

Justin Leonard won the US Amateur in 1992.

five consecutive birdies on the back nine on Saturday afternoon. John Harris and Justin Leonard were eleven strokes back. Tiger Woods was in fourth, twelve strokes behind.

Impressive from tee-to-green, Woods struggled on the difficult and challenging Sunnehanna greens. The young player missed several short putts much to the displeasure of the spectators who came to watch him play.

Sunday's round was little more than a formality, but Allen Doyle showed no signs of coasting. His final round of 66 established a new tournament record total of fourteen under-par 266, breaking Bobby Greenwood's eleven under par record total set in 1965. He became the first player in the 39-year history of the tournament to shoot four rounds under par. His thirteen shot margin of victory erased the previous record set in 1985 by Scott Verplank who won by seven strokes. Doyle amassed seventeen birdies over the final three rounds of golf on the usually challenging Sunnehanna layout.

He also became the second three-time champion of the Sunnehanna Amateur; the other was Jay Sigel.

"Allen is as good as any player we have playing in the amateur ranks right now," Sigel said. "He should be applauded. He ripped this golf course apart."

The only other player to break par was Steve Anderson, the Ohio Amateur and Public Links champion, who finished second. Jeff

Runner-up Steve Anderson

Kraemer, the Canadian Amateur champion from Bringham Young, and Justin Leonard, the Texas All-American, finished third, fourteen strokes behind. Tiger Woods shot a final round of 71 for a four-round total of 283 to finish seventeen strokes behind the champion.

Alen Doyle's performance came as close to perfection as anyone has ever come at Sunnehanna, making the 1992 Amateur the three most memorable days of golf in the tournament's history.

Sunnehanna Amateur
JAXON BRIGMAN

The 40th Sunnehanna Amateur began with the realization that it was, in all likelihood, the final appearance of Sunnehanna legend Jay Sigel. The three-time champion was making his 23rd appearance in the tournament. He first competed in the Sunnehanna Amateur in 1961, earning his first invitation by winning the 1960

Jaxon Brigman and caddie Brace Moran

Pennsylvania Junior. Sigel, Allen Doyle, and Tiger Woods were the most notable returnees from 1992.

Several of amateur golf's best young players were visiting Johnstown for the first time: Tim Herron from the University of New Mexico, and All-Americans Brian Gay from Florida, and Notah Begay from Stanford led the collegiate players.

Tim Herron's double bogey on the seventy-first hole cost him the title.

Another mid-amateur building an impressive resume was John Harris. In the summer of 1992, Harris reached the quarter-finals of the U.S. Amateur and finished runner-up in the Porter Cup.

The first round found a plethora of new names at the top of the scoreboard led by Mike Flynn from Texas Christian by way of Rochester, New Hampshire. Flynn shot 67 to lead by one stroke.

After 54 holes of play, Flynn remained in the lead with a three-round total of 207. One shot behind was Brian Gay and Tim Herron. Another stroke behind at 209 was defending champion Allen

Mike Flynn led for 63 holes

Doyle. Tiger Woods, a fifth place finisher the prior year, stood at 213 and tied for twelfth place. "I'm just not playing well," said Woods after three rounds. "My swing was just not there. It's as simple as that."

The ultimate winner of the tournament was determined more by squandered opportunities than by stellar play. Mike Flynn continued to lead after the front nine, but bogeyed four of his first five holes on the back-side, ending his hopes of winning.

"I really didn't play that bad on the back nine," said Flynn. "I hit a couple of putts too hard. I'm happy with the way the tournament went for me, but obviously I would've loved to have done better."

Jaxon Brigman

Gay birdied three of the first five holes. Then he double bogeyed six and eight after shanking his approach shot. "I don't know how to even explain number eight," Gay said.

A birdie on thirteen got Herron to three under par, but a double-bogey on seventeen derailed his march to the title. While the final pairing leaked oil all over the hilltop, Jaxon Brigman from Okla-homa State made his move after starting the day four shots off the pace.

Brian Gay finished tied for second with Tim Herrron.

An eagle on eleven and a birdie on twelve moved him to four under par, and into the lead which he never relinquished.

An additional birdie on sixteen by the native of Abilene, Texas, and Jaxon Brigman be-came the fourth Oklahoma State Cowboy to win the Sunnehanna Amateur.

"The Sunnehanna Amateur was my first amateur tournament and it was a very big tournament for me. It's obviulsy one of the biggest tournaments in amateur golf."
Tiger Woods

Sunnehanna Amateur
ALLEN DOYLE

Allen Doyle returned to Johnstown in 1994 hoping to become the first player to win four Sunnehanna Amateur titles. Jaxon Brigman, who was playing in his final amateur tournament, also returned to defend his title. Brigman was joined by Oklahoma State teammates and All-Americans Chris Tidland and Kris Cox.

Allen Doyle wins a fourth and final title.

Additional competition was expected to come from Walker Cup teammates John Harris, the 1993 U.S. Amateur champion, and Todd Demsey, the 1993 NCAA and Pacific Coast Amateur champion.

After an uneventful first day, Allen Doyle was positioned to win his fourth Sunnehanna Amateur title. The LaGrange, Georgia golfer led West Penn Amateur champion Sean Knapp, and University of Oklahoma standout Patrick Lee, by two strokes after 54 holes.

Pittsburgh standout, Sean Knapp, finished second.

Large crowds came to watch history being made as Doyle held off a final-round charge by Sean Knapp who closed within one shot of the leader, but it was Allen Doyle's day. He finished three strokes ahead of second place finisher Knapp, and five strokes ahead of Patrick Lee.

"This course is tailor made for him (Doyle)," playing partner Lee commented. "He just sees an opening to the green and he hits it right up there."

With his victory, Allen Doyle became the first four-time champion in the history of the nation's oldest 72-hole stroke play championship.

Sunnehanna Amateur

"This is a terrific tournament," Doyle said during the award ceremony on the eighteenth green. "I just would like to thank all of the people who came out here to watch us play."

Patrick Lee

Patrick Lee, Sean Knapp and Allen Doyle

Allen Doyle acknowledges the large crowd. Doyle reflected on his times in Johnstown. "The Sunnehanna Amateur was my first major amateur victory. Up until then all I had won were regional tournaments. The tournament put me on the top of the heap in terms of amateur golf." Of his four victories Doyle vivivdly recalled his record-setting victory in 1992. Doyle remembered, "The fouteenth hole I couldn't hold. My 5-wood rolled through the green and into the rough. From a tough lie I chipped in. The second time around my ball came-up short and I chipped in again for birdie. Tiger Woods looked at me and bowed. I have incredibly great memories of the Sunnehanna Amateur and the people of Jonhstown."

Sunnehanna Amateur
JOHN HARRIS

The sixty-six entrants were elated by the decision of Allen Doyle to turn professional. The LaGrange, Georgia native's reign had ended with his fourth title in six years in 1994. Amateur golf's best player's attempts to defeat Doyle at Sunnehanna had been futile.

Mid-amateurs considered likely to fill the void left by Jay Sigel and Allen Doyle were John Harris, Sean Knapp and Tim Jackson. In 1994, Jackson won the U.S. Mid-Amateur title and reached the quarter-finals of the U.S. Amateur.

For the first time in ten years an entire collegiate team, Oklahoma State, accepted invitations to the tournament. The Cowboys had just won the 1995 NCAA team title defeating Stanford on the first playoff hole. The team was led by first team All-Americans Alan Bratton, a two-time Big Eight champion, and Chris Tidland and included Kris Cox, Brian Guetz, and Tripp Kuehne.

Other All-Americans who entered the tournament were Notah Begay from Stanford and Patrick Lee from Oklahoma. Lee finished third in the 1994 Sunnehanna Amateur.

John Harris

Oklahoma State All-American and runner-up Kris Cox.

Notah Begay finished fourth. He was the first Native American member of the Walker Cup team.

Sunnehanna Amateur

Oklahoma State All-American Alan Bratton finished third.

After the first day's play, the scoreboard looked like the Cowboy Invitational as three golfers from Stillwater were in the top five. Kris Cox led after an opening round score of 66, aided by a back nine 31. College players seemed ready to reassert there domination of the tournament. Cox was followed by Tripp Kuehne, Notah Begay, and Tulsa standout Dennis Hillman with 67. Alan Bratton and J.J. Henry were two strokes behind with rounds of 68.

After 36 more holes of golf, John Harris was perched atop the leader board. Harris added back-to-back rounds of 65 to his opening 69 to lead the tournament by two strokes. The 1993 U.S. Amateur champion had, by his own admission, played good rounds of golf at Sunnehanna, but never had a good tournament. Opening round leader Kris Cox recovered from a second round 71 with a third round 64 to stand two strokes behind Harris. Alan Bratton was in third, another two strokes behind his teammate.

The tournament came down to the final hole with John Harris maintaining a two stroke lead. After splitting the fairway with his tee shot, Harris' approach shot spun off the green and into the heavy rough. Cox drove into the rough between two fairway bunkers, then made a remarkable recovery shot that cleared a greenside bunker, finishing five feet from the pin.

After Harris missed his par putt, Cox was given the opportunity to force extra holes. It was not to be as the native of Lafayette, Louisiana watched his birdie slide by. With his victory, John Harris became the sixth U.S. Amateur champion to win the Sunnehanna Amateur.

John Harris

Sunnehanna Amateur
JEFF THOMAS

T he field of sixty entrants included only thirteen players with prior experience in the tournament. John Harris returned to defend his title, his competition was expected to come from a bevy of talented young players.

'96

Ryuji Imada, the 1995 Porter Cup champion and the nation's top-ranked junior was considered a likely challenger for the title. Imada, the third ranked amateur in the nation, captured the Azalea Amateur in the spring of 1996.

Jeff Thomas

Another youngster making his first appearance in Johnstown was 18-year-old Steve Scott. Scott, who had just completed his freshman year at the University of Florida, reached the semi-finals of the U.S. Amateur in 1995 and qualified for the 1996 U.S Open.

Other top collegiate players who accepted invitations were J.J. Henry and John Curley Henry, the two-time Connecticut Amateur champion who played at Texas Christian. Curley, from Florida Southern, finished runner-up in the recently completed NCAA Division II Championship. He finished eighth in the 1995 Sunnehanna Amateur.

J.J. Henry plays while Jeff Thomas looks on.

The first day, high winds and hard, fast greens put the field on the defensive. By day's end, no players managed to break par, a tournament first. The greens gave everyone trouble, but Ted Purdy's ninth hole putting woes were unforgettable lying three on the par five. Purdy hit what was a seemingly perfect putt with just the right speed but narrowly missed. Left with a two-footer for par, he missed again leaving another putt of the same distance. A backhanded effort missed again leaving him with a five-footer. He missed that as well. When he was finally done, Purdy had a five putt triple bogey eight. Purdy recovered from misadventure to shoot three over par 73, his ninth hole prevented him from leading the tournament.

J.J. Henry chips on eighteen

After the conclusion of Saturday's rounds, J.J Henry and Purdy led the tournament. Jeff Thomas, the eight-time New Jersey Amateur champion and the 1993 U.S. Mid- Amateur champion was a single stroke back followed by John Curley.

Jeff Thomas' thoughts on the final tee were, "Play it safe", needing only a par to win the tournament. Thomas then pulled a seven-wood into the left rough. A nine-iron finished short of the green and a pitch shot left him a five-foot putt for the championship. Calmly, the South Plainfield native drained the putt.

Throughout the day other players frittered away opportunities to win the tournament. J.J. Henry missed a four-foot birdie putt on the fourth hole and later, with a chance to tie Thomas, from the same distance on the seventeenth hole. Henry bogeyed the final hole to finish two-strokes behind the winner.

Steve Scott fired one of only three sub-par rounds on the final day, but bogeyed the seventeenth hole. It was the difference between himself and Thomas.

Ted Purdy could only sit and think what might have been reliving his first day foray on the ninth hole. Purdy finished two strokes behind Thomas. His final round of 74 tied him for third with Henry, Ryuji Imada, and Soon Ko.

Ted Purdy

Sunnehanna Amateur

DUKE DELCHER

A strong contingent of mid-amateurs returned to Johnstown in 1997. Former champions Jeff Thomas and John Harris were joined by Jerry Courville, Duke Delcher, and Buddy Marucci, looking to continue the recent success of the older sect at Sunnehanna.

Duke Delcher

Visiting Sunnehanna for the final time was J.J. Henry, a third place finisher the prior year, as well as runner-up Steve Scott.

In 1996, Scott finished runner-up to Tiger Woods in the U.S. Amateur in one of the most memorable matches in the rich history of the nation's amateur championship.

After the completion of the first days play Tripp Kuehne, runner-up in the 1994 U.S. Amateur, and Duke Delcher were tied for the lead at two under par.

On Saturday, tournament veterans continued there success. Patience, a key component of

Jerry Courville

success at Sunnehanna was Duke Delcher's mantra throughout his first 54 holes. Knowing that par was a good score, Delcher followed a morning round of 70 with an exceptional second round of 66 to lead Aaron Oberholser by one stroke.

Oberholser, an All-American from San Jose State, followed an opening round of 71 with back-to-back rounds of 67. John Harris, with three rounds of 69, was three

Aaron Oberholser

strokes behind and in third place.

Entering the final round, Duke Delcher knew that a victory at Sunnehanna could possibly secure his best-last opportunity to make the Walker Cup team. After four holes, Oberholser had overtaken Delcher and led outright. Later, John Harris, after a front nine of 34, assumed the lead for three holes.

Ahead of the final group, John Rollins went on a birdie tear making birdies on fifteen, sixteen and seventeen then bogeyed the final hole to end his chance. Delcher, after a

John Rollins

difficult front nine, righted himself with birdies on ten and eleven while Harris played passively on the backside.

The tournament was decided on the final two holes as Delcher finished birdie-birdie to win the title by three strokes over John Harris and by four strokes over third place finishers Aaron Oberholser and John Rollins.

John Harris finished runner-up,

154

Sunnehanna Amateur

STEVE SHEEHAN

T he tournament field was dominated by mid-amateurs as many of the nation's top collegiate players either weren't invited or elected to forego the tournament.

Among the top returnees were defending champion Duke Delcher and third place finisher Aaron Oberholser, the nation's sixth-ranked.

Steve Sheehan

Many of the best mid-amateurs accepted invitations and included Jerry Courville, Paul Simson, and Bert Atkinson, the two-time South Carolina Amateur champion and 1997 Rice Planters champion. In 1997, Simson finished runner-up in the North-South Amateur and Northeast Amateur.

The top collegiate players were Sunnehanna regular Steve Scott from Florida, Michael Boyd from the University of Tulsa, and Edward Loar from Oklahoma State. Boyd was the highest ranked amateur in the field. The Tulsa, Oklahoma golfer won the 1997 Monroe Invitational and was a quarter-finalist in the U.S. Amateur. Loar, a second-team All-American, won the 1997 Southwestern Amateur.

The first day produced an unlikely leader, Steve Sheehan, the Nevada Stroke and Match Play champion. Sheehan led the tournament after a bogey-free opening round of 65.

Five players were tied at 3-under-par 67 and included Bert Atkinson, Trip Kuehne, Doug LaBelle, Len Johnsen, and Joey Maxon. Eleven golfers broke par the first day.

Robert Gerwin's day ended eleven hours and 35 minutes after it started with the 54-hole lead. The reigning Ohio Amateur Champion passed the opening round leader Steve Sheehan after impressive rounds of 67-65. Sheehan trailed the new leader by two strokes.

Also noteworthy was the play of four-time West Virginia Amateur champion Pat Carter. Playing with Gerwin, Carter shot a course record back nine score of seven under-par 28.

On the final day, bogeys were an exception rather than a rule as twenty players broke par on Sunday. At the tournament's end, 15 golfers in the 61-player field had finished under-par for the tournament.

Gerwin, a quarter-finalist in the 1997 U.S. Amateur, continued his fine

Sunnehanna Amateur

Runner-up Robert Gerwin led after sixty-three holes.

play on Sunday ending the front nine with a four-stroke lead. One hole later the momentum changed dramatically. On the tenth hole, Sheehan drained a 35-foot birdie putt while Gerwin bogeyed, shaving two strokes from the Cincinnati golfer's lead.

Sheehan's added birdies on eleven and twelve to close the gap by another stroke, as Gerwin matched his birdie on twelve. After watching Gerwin waste birdie opportunities on fifteen, sixteen, and seventeen, Sheehan responded by draining an 18-foot birdie on seventeen to tie for the lead. After 72-holes of golf, a playoff ensued.

After routine pars on the first hole, Gerwin missed the green on the second playoff hole, landed in a greenside bunker. He then hit a fine bunker shot that finished three feet from the hole, then watched as Sheehan 2-putt for par and prepared to play the eighteenth hole again. Gerwin's putt burned the right edge for a bogey five.

Steve Sheehan did not come to the 45th Sunnehanna Amateur with the pedigree of many of the other players in the tournament. It was Sheehan's first opportunity to compete in a major amateur tournament. Sheehan was not a collegiate star, nor had he tried the professional life. In fact, he had quit the game at the age of 19 and did not play for fourteen years.

But the play of another member of his family brought him back to the game. His sister, Patty Sheehan, dominated professional woman's golf in the late 1980's and early 1990's. Steve was inspired to play again after witnessing, among her many victories, her two U.S. Women's Open titles,

Pat Carter

Sunnehanna Amateur
William V. Price
A Long Time Chairman

Bill Price's tenure as Sunnehanna Amateur chairman ended after 29 years of remarkable service in 1998. Price joined the committee in 1965; two years later he was named Co-Chairman with Dr. Hampton Corson. In 1969, he became sole chairman and oversaw the continued growth of the tournament. Price's professional leadership and unerring demand for quality made an invitation to the Sunnehanna Amateur one of the toughest and most prized in amateur golf.

Invitations were earned not given. "I remember it was years until I could get in," Jay Sigel recalled. Yet, Sigel respected the high standards that were expected to get an invitation, "It was the most difficult invitational to get into. When you don't have the credentials, you don't get in."

Mr. and Mrs. William V. Price

Just as he expected a certain standard from the players for an invitation, Price demanded the same standards from himself. To achieve his annual goal of having the nation's best tournament, he and wife Carlyn traveled to events throughout the country. Ben Crenshaw recalled, "You'd be somewhere else, playing, and the next thing you knew, Mr. Price was there saying "hello." He spread a lot of goodwill for Sunnehanna that way, and it was passed along by the players, by word of mouth."

He devoted endless hours to the Sunnehanna Amateur paying attention to every detail. From housing, to travel, to meals, Price wanted to ensure that the Sunnehanna Amateur was the best in every way possible. When it came to the players, Price had an encyclopedic memory.

"I thought he was the best," said Allen Doyle, the four-time champion of the Sunnehanna Amateur. "He never forgot a name, he never forgot where you lived. He had all the details of when people were arriving." Doyle recalled his first trip to Sunnehanna in 1984: "The first time I played there, I drove up and I mis-figured the time of the ride to get there. I got there at 3:30 after I figured I'd be there at noon."

"He said, 'I thought you were getting here at 12.' I don't think there is a detail that he didn't know." It was William Price's special attention to details that made the Sunnehanna Amateur what it is.

With all of the demands of the Sunnehanna Amateur, Price managed to also find time to devote to the Western Pennsylvania Golf Association. His expertise and knowledge was gratefully appreciated. In 1996, *Golf Journal*, the publication of the USGA, acknowledged the significant contributions to golf by several tournament chairmen including Bill Price.

William Price set a standard for future chairman that will be impossible to match. His legacy of excellence lives on every June with playing of the Sunnehanna Amateur.

Sunnehanna Amateur

EDWARD LOAR

From 1970 through 1987 mid-amateurs' efforts to win the Sunnehanna Amateur were fruitless. With the exception of Bob Zender in 1971 and Jay Sigel in 1976 and 1978, college players dominated tournament play.

This began to change with Jay Sigel's victory in 1988, followed by Allen Doyle's four titles in six years.

Four straight victories by four different mid-ams made them the pre-tournament favorites, and 1999 was no exception.

In 1998 Mid-Ams dominated amateur golf: Tim Jackson won the North & South Amateur title; Gene Elliott, the Porter Cup; and Bert Atkinson, the Rice Planters. Other prominent mid-ams included Sean Knapp, Danny Green, and Tom McKnight who was runner-up in 1998 U.S. Amateur. Previous champions Steve Sheehan, Duke Delcher, and John Harris hoped to win their second titles.

Edward Loar won back-to-back titles in 1999 and 2000 .

A small group of college players included Steve Scott from Florida, and Oklahoma State teammates Charles Howell and Edward Loar. A late addition to the tournament was Lucas Glover from Clemson.

Lucas Glover quickly made an impression on the field firing an opening round of 64. Close behind was Edward Loar, who shot a tourna-

Lucas Glover first round leader in 1999

ment front nine record of 30. The native of Rockwall, Texas, made bogeys on eleven and twelve before rebounding with birdies on fifteen and eighteen to shoot 65. Sean Knapp, Matt Call, Pat Carter, and Charles Howell were all tied at three under-par 67. Nine players broke par the first day.

Edward Loar passed first round leader Glover with a morning round with a four under-par 66. Loar continued his fine play in the afternoon getting as low as ten under par for the tournament until cooling off with a third-round score of 70.

Sunnehanna Amateur

Seven strokes behind with one round to play were Charles Howell and Sean Knapp. First-round leader Glover and defending champion Steve Sheehan were the only other players below par after three rounds.

When asked how to catch the leader, Sean Knapp responded with a smile and said, "Maybe if someone takes him out in the parking lot." Knapp knew it would be difficult to catch the long-hitting, left-handed Texan.

Edward Loar displayed a deft touch from around the greens.

Loar eliminated any chance that someone could catch him with birdies on nine, ten and eleven. As the Texan reached eleven under-par, thoughts soon switched to Allen Doyle's seemingly unattainable record score of 266. Bogeys on the twelfth and thirteenth holes eliminated any chance of the record being reached. Edward Loar's final margin of victory was five strokes over college roommate Charles Howell and Tim Jackson.

While Howell didn't win the tournament, he accomplished something of a milestone reaching the 575-yard par 5 ninth hole three straight rounds in two. Only three players had reached the green in two before: Lance TenBroeck, Dan Pohl, and Fred Couples.

After the final round, the Oklahoma State roommates praised each other's play. "We've seen each others best and worst," Howell said. "He's a great player and he played good this week."

The 1999 champion also had compliments for his friend and roommate, "I love playing with Charles, he's a great player, we had a good time out there today," said Loar. "For us to finish one and two, I think, says a lot about our program."

Edward Loar age 11 and Charles Howell age 10 at the 1989 Future Masters Tournament in Dothan, Alabama. Ten years later the Oklahoma State teammates finished first and second in the Sunnehanna Amateur.

Sunnehanna Amateur

In June 2000, Edward Loar returned to defend his title against a field that included nine of the top ten finishers from the previous year. The defending champion's principle competition was expected to again come from his Oklahoma State teammate Charles Howell. Howell had won both the 2000 NCAA and Big 12 Conference titles by record-setting margins.

Other contenders for the title included All-Americans Lucas Glover from Clemson, Kyle Thompson from the University of South Carolina, and Alex Rocha from Mississippi State.

After the first day's play, Loar and Howell were atop the leader board just as the year before. They were joined by Michael Beard and Tom McKnight with opening rounds of 68.

After 54 holes, Loar remained in the lead for the sixth straight round at Sunnehanna. Three strokes behind Loar were Sean Knapp, Erik Compton, James Driscoll, and David Eger.

Playing in the same three-some, Eger and Compton closed their afternoon rounds with identical back nines of 32, and rounds of 67 and 68, respectively. Sean Knapp recovered from an opening round of 74 with the best two rounds on Saturday. The Pittsburgh golfer fired rounds of 67 and 69 to get into contention.

"It's great to be leading, but when you look at the board there are quite a few guys in the hunt," Loar commented at the end of the day's play. He knew he had a lot of golf ahead of him and fine players chasing him.

Over the final eighteen holes, the momentum changed numerous times. Loar held onto a two-stroke lead with five holes to play. On fourteen, Compton's approach shot on the 227-yard par 3 finished three feet from the pin. He made his putt and closed within one stroke of Loar.

Next, Eger birdied both fifteen and sixteen to become co-leader. He failed to take the outright lead on seventeen, missing his putt from eight feet.

James Driscoll

Charles Howell 2000 NCAA Champion.

160

Sunnehanna Amateur

On the final hole, Loar missed the green with a wedge. Compton's approach shot finished 30 feet from the pin. Eger, who played first, executed a spectacular shot from a horrendous lie to eight feet of the hole. Loar recovered from his poor wedge, playing a remarkable flop-shot to three feet of the hole, seemingly assuring a par. Compton then drained his birdie putt to tie Loar.

Eger, with a chance to win outright, watched his birdie effort miss and Loar made his par-saving putt. After 72-holes of play, the tournament embarked on its first three-man playoff in the Amateur's history.

Returning to the eighteenth hole, Eger was quickly eliminated after making a bogey. Loar missed the green again with a wedge, his ball finishing in almost the identical location he found himself just 20 minutes earlier. Again he saved par, this time making a ten-foot putt. Both players tied the next two play-off holes with pars.

Playing the eighteenth hole for the fourth time in an hour, Loar again aimed at an imaginary hole to the right of the green. Compton hit his approach shot from 165 yards into a greenside bunker. Loar, whose pitch shot finished ten feet of the cup, watched Compton belly his bunker shot, the ball barely on the green and 35 feet from the cup.

After Loar missed his putt for par to win the tournament, Compton faced a four-foot putt to force another hole. It was not to be. Edward Loar became the Sunnehanna Amateur's third back-to-back champion joining Scott Verplank and Allen Doyle.

Over the final two weeks of his amateur career, Edward Loar was a part of two playoff victories: Oklahoma State's team championship over Georgia Tech and his win at Sunnehanna.

"To successfully defend my title is a great honor, and to end my career on a winning note is fantastic." Loar said. "It's just a great way for myself to go out on top."

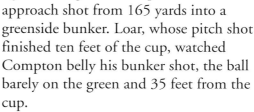

Erik Compton reacts to his long birdie putt on eighteen.

David Eger finished runner-up

Sunnehanna Amateur
LUCAS GLOVER

The 48th Sunnehanna Amateur had its strongest field since the late 1970's. Nine of the top eleven players from the prior year returned, and the field included many of most of the nation's top college players.

Erik Compton, 2000 runner-up, was joined by fellow University of Georgia

Lucas Glover celebrates his title with mother, Hershey, and grandfather, Dick Hendley.

teammates and All-Americans Ryan Hybl, Nick Cassini, Bryant Odom, and David Miller. Lucas Glover brought Clemson teammate and fellow first-team All-American John Engler, and D.J. Trahan. Trahan was the nation's top-ranked amateur and reigning U.S Public Links champion. Also adding luster to the field were foreign players Jamie Elson from Augusta State via Warwickshire, England, and Jon Mills from Kent State and Brocklin, Ontario, Canada. Both were college All-Americans. Elson was considered a leading candidate for the Great Britain and Ireland side for the Walker Cup after finishing runner-up in the 2000 NCAA championships.

The first day, players took advantage of a soft course as seventeen contestants in the field of 71 equaled or broke par on the vulnerable course. By the day's end, John Engler, a two-time first-team All-American, led James Driscoll, runner-up in the 2000 U.S. Amateur, by one stroke after an opening round of 66.

The trend of low scores continued the following day as thirteen players broke par, and six players equaled par in the morning round. Lucas Glover took the 36-hole lead, adding 65 to a first-day round of 67.

In the afternoon, James Driscoll took the lead. The University of Virginia golfers got as low as nine under par only to throw strokes away coming home. Paired with Engler and Glover, Driscoll recorded a disastrous quadruple-bogey on the fourteenth and came back to the field. Glover added an even-par round to his stanza to take the lead. First-round leader Engler recovered from a morning round of

John Engler led after the first round and eventually finished third.

72 with a 68.

Another story on Saturday was the play of Chris Mundorf of North Carolina State. Mundorf, the 2000 Cardinal Amateur champion, followed an opening round of 71 with a two under par score of 68. In the afternoon, the Raleigh native shot 33 on his front nine. On the back nine made four birdies to shoot six under-par 64.

Four of the top five players on the leader board came from the Atlantic Coast Conference, with Brigham Young's Billy Harvey joining Engler and Driscoll who were three strokes behind co-leaders Glover and Mundorf.

After several days of warm, sunny weather, the course began to dry out, making birdies more difficult to come by. After the front nine Glover maintained a one-stroke lead over Mundorf, and was two strokes ahead of Harvey. On eleven, Glover reached the easy par-5 in two with an 8-iron then three-putted from 45 feet. On the same hole, Mundorf missed a modest three-foot birdie putt after a scintillating long bunker shot. Annoyed with his effort on eleven, Mundorf came back with a birdie on the twelfth hole.

Glover responded to his good friend's birdie with a birdie of his own from 20 feet on fourteen to reclaim the lead. Chris Mundorf made another birdie from 40 feet on sixteen. It was Mundorf's last time at the top.

On the next hole, the North Carolina State golfer narrowly missed the green to the left, then pitched to three feet of the cup. His putt for par took an untimely bounce on the way to the hole and he made bogey. On the final hole, Mundorf, consistently out-driven by 40 yards all day, drove into the left rough. He gouged his iron shot from the heavy grass to 70 feet from the cup.

Mundorf's improbable cross-country effort missed, and Glover wrapped up his victory by making a birdie.

With his mother, Hershey, and grandfather, Dick Hendley, watching every shot, Lucas Glover became the 48th champion of the Sunnehanna Amateur. For Glover, the three-time South Carolina Amateur champion, his third trip to Johnstown was a charm and gave him the title he had coveted since his first visit.

The quality of the field was confirmed later that summer as Lucas Glover, along with six other Sunnehanna competitors, were named to the ten-man U.S. Walker Cup team. Jamie Elson, also made tournament history, becoming the first contestant to play for the Great Britain and Ireland side in the Walker Cup.

Chris Mundorf putts while Billy Harvey watches.

Sunnehanna Amateur

DILLARD PRUITT

Only four of the top ten players from 2001 returned to Johnstown for the 49th Sunnehanna Amateur. Tournament veterans Tripp Davis, Danny Green, Sean Knapp, and Pat Carter were joined by several of the nation's best college players. Among them first-team All-Americans D.J. Trahan from Clemson, and Hunter Mahan from Oklahoma State, the 1999 U.S. Junior champion. Trahan, the 2002 Azalea Amateur champion, was named recipient of the Ben Hogan Award given to the nation's top college player.

Dillard Pruitt won his second Sunnehanna Amateur title nineteen years after his first victory.

Among the first-time competitors considered likely contenders included All-Americans Brendan DeJonge, the former Zimbabwe Amateur champion from Virginia Tech; Lee Williamson, the 2001 Indiana Amateur and Open champion from Purdue University; Justin Walters from Johannesburg, South Africa and North Carolina State; and Troy Matteson, the recent winner of the NCAA individual title from Georgia Tech.

Danny Green was the leader most of the day after shooting an opening round of 66. Tripp Davis, who teed off just as Green was finishing his round, came in later that day with the same score. One stroke behind the leaders was Greg Jones of Clemson followed by DeJonge, Garth Mulroy, and Adam Rubinson, who shot two under par 68.

Lee Williamson Purdue All-American

Low scores were abundant Saturday and at day's end and Tripp Davis' methodical approach prevailed. The Norman, Oklahoma golf course architect added rounds of 68 and 69 to his opening round of 66 to lead the tournament by a single stroke. In the afternoon, Davis had been as low as eight under-par for the tournament after four consecutive birdies on holes eleven through fourteen, but a double-bogey on seventeen marred a great day.

The lowest score on Saturday afternoon was shot by Lee Williams, who shot a record-tying score of 63. Williams' score tied him with Bobby Greenwood, Bob Zender, Charles Kunkle, and Skip Alexander. Zender and Greenwood had used their

Sunnehanna Amateur

Hunter Mahan, the nation's top collegiate player, led with nine holes to play.

record rounds to catapult themselves toward the title. The Auburn University golfer hoped for the same as his 63 coupled with his first two rounds of 72 and 73 put Williams five behind Davis.

Hunter Mahan opened his afternoon round with four consecutive birdies on the front nine. After fifteen holes, he stood at seven under par, but a bogey on sixteen, followed by pars on the final two holes, left him one shot short of tying the course record. His round of 64, added to a pair of 70's put him one stroke behind Davis. Another stroke behind was Dillard Pruitt. A former winner on the PGA tour, Pruitt had not played any competitive golf since 1996.

On the final day, Hunter Mahan shot a fine three under par front nine score of 33 to take the lead over both Davis and Pruitt. Then astonishingly, the Oklahoma State standout came unglued. After a double-bogey on the tenth hole, Mahan staggered home with a backside score of 41.

Tripp Davis took the lead and was comfortably in control of the tournament with four holes to go. Then Davis' wheels came off, making bogeys on three of the final four holes to fall back and tie Dillard Pruitt, who closed with a respectable final round of 70. The first four-hole aggregate playoff in the tournament's history was needed to determine the champion.

The playoff was anti-climactic. A devastated Davis was unable to recover from his disastrous finish. Four pars were all that were needed by Dillard Pruitt to win his second Sunnehanna title.

For Pruitt, it had been an amazing three days. His return to Sunnehanna was made possible after running into his caddy from 1983, Tom Szwast, while officiating the Pennsylvania Classic at Laurel Valley the prior year. Szwast suggested Pruitt contact the committee about participating in the tournament, which he did. Pruitt then coaxed his former caddy out of retirement.

Tripp Davis stumbled down the stretch.

Nineteen years later, the former Clemson Tiger celebrated his second Sunnehanna Amateur title. "I can't believe it happened, I really can't. It feels great," the ecstatic 40 year-old said. "This is so much sweeter than the last one. I respect the game a lot more now than I did then and for this to happen to me this week is pretty special. I'm so much happier with myself this time. At 40 years old, winning an amateur tournament like this? I never thought that would happen."

Sunnehanna Amateur
MATT HENDRIX

*T*he 50th anniversary of the Sunnehanna Amateur could have been titled "Back to the Future."

'03 The smallest field in ten years, 58 players, had the largest number of entrants from Pennsylvania (seven) since the inaugural tournament. Arnold Palmer, the 1948 Sunnehanna Invitational champion, could be found walking the course as a spectator. Palmer's grandson, Sam Saunders, coompeted in his first Sunnehanna Amateur.

Matt Hendrix became the third straight Clemson Tiger to win the tournament.

Defending champion, Dillard Pruitt, congratulated fellow Clemson Tigers Greg Jones, Jack Ferguson, and Matt Hendrix on winning Clemson's first NCAA golf team title. Two All-Americans, Brandt Snedeker from Vanderbilt and Justin Smith from the University of Minnesota's accepted invitations. Snedeker, a first team All-American in 2003, was a second team All-American and the U.S. Public Links champion in 2002. Smith, from Moon Township, Pennsylvania was third team All-American and an integral member of Minnesota's national championship team in 2002. A coup for the tournament was the arrival of Alejandro Canizares. The son Jose Maria Canizares the outstanding Spanish touring professional. Canizares enrolled at Arizona State University in January and won the 2003 NCAA individual crown.

Danny Green led after the first day.

The first day the rain held off held off, and Kevin Larsen led the tournament. With 66 one stroke ahead of Danny Green and Jay Mundy.

The second day, Mother Nature was the winner as rain pelted the course in the morning permitting only 27 holes of golf to be played. At days end, Justin Smith was the leader. Smith

Sunnehanna Amateur

Pennsylvanian Justin Smith finished second.

added rounds of 67 and a nine hole round of three under par to his opening score of 69 to lead Matt Hendrix by two strokes.

Smith maintained a two-shot lead after completion of the third round. The Pennsylvanian continued to show fine form early in the fourth round. Smith birdied the first hole and at one point widened his lead to four strokes, but then made bogeys on the eighth and ninth to come back to Matt Hendrix. Hendrix ended his nine with a birdie to shrink Smith's lead to one stroke. The outcome of the tournament was determined on the twelfth hole. Both players missed the green, Smith's ball finishing in the bunker, Hendrix's ball in the sticky rough. Hendrix holed his difficult downhill chip shot. " That chip in on 12 was the one that put him over the edge because we were both treading water there for a while." said Justin Smith, "He made that, then he birdied fourteen. He was playing really well. He deserved to win."

Matt Hendrix fine final round of 67

Clemson's Greg Jones finished third.

defeated Justin Smith by two strokes. Clemson teammate, Greg Jones, who finished fifth the year before, finished third five strokes behind his teammate. Hendrix victory was the third straight victory by a Clemson Tiger at Sunnehanna. "It's kind of too sweet." said an obviously elated Hendrix afterward," If you would have told me we were going to win a national championship then come up here and win Sunnehanna, I'd say you're crazy..

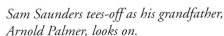

Sam Saunders tees-off as his grandfather, Arnold Palmer, looks on.

Champions
of the
Sunnehanna Amateur

1954 Don Cherry	1979 John Cook
1955 Hillman Robbins	1980 Bobby Clampett
1956 Gene Dahlbender	1981 Jodie Mudd
1957 Joe Campbell	1982 Brad Faxon
1958 William Hyndman	1983 Dillard Pruitt
1959 Thomas Aaron	1984 Scott Verplank
1960 Gene Dahlbender	1985 Scott Verplank
1961 Richard Siderowf	1986 Billy Andrade
1962 Dr Edgar Updegraff	1987 Greg Lesher
1963 Roger McManus	1988 Jay Sigel
1964 Gary Cowan	1989 Allen Doyle
1965 Bobby Greenwood	1990 Allen Doyle
1966 Jack Lewis Jr.	1991 Paul Claxton
1967 William Hyndman	1992 Allen Doyle
1968 Bobby Greenwood	1993 Jaxon Brigman
1969 Leonard Thompson	1994 Allen Doyle
1970 Howard Twitty	1995 John Harris
1971 Bob Zender	1996 Jeff Thomas
1972 Mark Hayes	1997 Duke Delcher
1973 Ben Crenshaw	1998 Steve Sheehan
1974 Dave Strawn	1999 Edward Loar
1975 Jamie Gonzales	2000 Edward Loar
1976 Jay Sigel	2001 Lucas Glover
1977 John Cook	2002 Dillard Pruitt
1978 Jay Sigel	2003 Matt Hendrix

Champions of the Sunnehanna
Invitational

1936 Dr Joseph McHugh	1946 Bill Haverstick
1937 Dr Joseph McHugh	1947 Buddy Lutz
1938 Earl Hewitt	1948 Arnold Palmer
1939 William Lewis	1949 Buddy Lutz
1940 Cecil McClain	1950 Charles Kunkle Jr.
1941 Steve Kovach	1951 Jack Benson
1942-1945	
Suspended due to World War II	

Sunnehanna Notables

Club Presidents

1920-1927	L. R. Custer
1928	Telford Lewis
1929-1933	Michael J. Bracken
1934	Robert S. Waters
1935-1942	Wilson Slick
1943	W. R. Suppes
1944-1946	H. V. Brown
1947-1949	James W. Ashcom
1950	E. W. Overdorff
1951	D. J. W. Lynam
1952	W. J. Cahill
1953	S. D. Evans
1954	Ralph Willett
1955	Charles W. Kunkle, Jr.
1956	Howard M. Picking, Jr.
1957 (01-04)	William D. Mac Donnell
1957	Dr. George F. Wheeling (elec 4/23)
1958	Andrew J. Fisher
1959	Parker R. Lawson
1960	G. F. Edwards
1961	L. Homer Chalfant
1962	Frank O. Phillips
1963	A. Hugh Wagner
1964	Wayne G. Wolfe, Esq.
1965	Robert M. Smith
1966-1967	Charles S. Price
1968	N. Gwynne Dodson
1969	Dr. Hampton P. Corson
1970	Fred E. Cunningham
1971	Byron K. Custer, Jr.
1972-1973	Robert G. Rose, Esq.
1974-1975	Dr. J. B. Lovette
1976	Theodore W. Biddle
1977-1978	Richard B. Edwards
1979	James O. Whelan, Jr.
1980	William E. Kirwan
1981	J. Phillips Saylor
1982	James Dewar
1983-1984	William Crooks
1985	Dr. Robert Tomhave
1986	Alvin Glosser
1987	Gary Horner
1988	Frederick Mickel
1989	Samuel J. Catanese
1990	Dr. Richard McKinley
1991	J. Phillips Saylor
1992-1993	Dr. Patrick Wolfe
1994	James R. Walsh
1995	Gary S. Platt
1996	Donald Overdorff
1997	Denver E. Wharton
1998	Michael Wolfe
1999	Gary Horner
2000	Jim Sharer
2001	Charles Price, III
2002	Robert Smeal
2003	George Wolfe
2004	Tom Stephenson

Head Professionals

1921-1936	Bert Battell
1937-1944	Morrie Gravat
1946-1949	Carl Beljan
1950-1956	Bob Gutwein
1956-1958	Eddie Thompson
1959	Bob Keller
1960-1964	Dick Masterson
1965-1982	John Goettlicher
1983-present	Joe Shorto

Players

1961 Walker Cup Team:(l-r) R.E. Cochran, Dr. F.M Taylor, C.R. Coe, D.R. Beman, E.S. Andrews, J. Westland (non plaing captain), H. Hyndman III, D.R. Cherry, R.W. Gardner, J.W. Nicklaus, C.B. Smith

Tommy Aaron
Buddy Alexander
Don Allen
Billy Andrade
Doug Ballenger
Notah Begay
Deane Beman
Ted Bishop
Mike Brannan
Alan Bratton
George Burns
Clark Burroughs
Bill Campbell
Joe Campbell
Nick Cassini
Ron Cerrudo
Dick Chapman
Don Cherry*
Ron Commons
Jerry Courville,Jr.
Kris Cox
Bruce Cudd
Duke Delcher
Todd Demsey
Allen Doyle*
James Driscoll
David Duval
Dan Edwards
David Eger
Chick Evans
Brad Faxon*
Doug Fischesser
Marty Fleckman
John Fought
Frank Fuhrer
James Gabrielson
Robert Gamez
Brian Gay
Vinnie Giles
James Grant
Danny Green
Lucas Glover
Jay Haas
Gary Hallberg
John Harris*

Vance Heafner
Matt Hendrix
Tim Herron
Scott Hoch
Jim Holtgrieve
Mark Hopkins
Ralph Howe
Bill Hyndman
Joe Inman
Tim Jackson
Kevin Johnson
Tripp Kuehne
Gary Koch
Franklin Langham

Randy Leen
Justin Leonard
Greg Lesher
Bob Lewis
Jack Lewis
Edward Loar
Bill Loeffler
Davis Love III
Buddy Marucci
Doug Martin
Len Mattiace
Bob May
Billy Mayfair
Tom McKnight

Steve Melnyk
Phil Mickelson
Allen Miller
John Miller
Lindy Miller
Dale Morey
Jodie Mudd
Bob Murphy
Jack Nicklaus
Billy Joe Patton
Mark Pfeil
Mike Podolak
Lee Porter
Joe Rassett
Fred Ridley
Hillman Robbins
William Rogers
Adam Rubinson
Steve Scott*
Richard Siderowf
Jay Sigel
Scott Simpson
Charles Smith
Randy Sonnier
Jim Sorenson
Mike Sposa
Craig Stadler
Curtis Strange
Hal Sutton
Dick Von Tacky
David Tentis
D. J. Trahan
Ed Tutwiler
Ed Updegraff
Scott Verplank
Lanny Wadkins
Marty West
Ward Wettlaufer
Jason Widener
Lee Wiiliams
Casey Wittenberg
Willie Wood
Tiger Woods
Danny Yates
George Zahringer

1973 Walker Cup Team:(l-r) Back Row, G. Koch, D. Eswards, M.Pfeil, W. Rogers, D. Ballinger, J.W. Sweetster (non playing captain),Front Row, M.Killian, M.M. Giles III, R.L. Siderowf, M.R. West III

Players

Major Championships Winners

The Masters Champions

Tommy Aaron
Fred Couples
Ben Crenshaw
Phil Mickleson
Jack Nicklaus
Arnold Palmer
Craig Stadler
Art Wall, Jr.
Tiger Woods

*Phil Mickelson
2004 Masters
Champion*

U.S. Open Champions

Julius Boros
Charles Evans,Jr.
Jim Furyk
Hubert Green
Lee Janzen
Steve Jones
Jack Nicklaus
Andy North
Arnold Palmer
Scott Simpson
Curtis Strange
Tiger Woods

*Curtis Strange,
1992,1993 US Open*

PGA Champions

Julius Boros
Mark Brooks
Steve Elkington
Hubert Green
Davis Love III
John Mahaffey
Jack Nicklaus
Jeff Sluman
Hal Sutton
Bob Tway
Lanny Wadkins
Tiger Woods

*Steve Elkington
1995 PGA Champion*

British Open Champions

David Duval
Tom Lehman
Justin Leonard
Jack Nicklaus
Arnold Palmer
Bill Rogers
Tiger Woods

*Justin Leonard
1997 British Open*

*Lee Janzen
1993 US Open*

*Andy North
US Open*

*Jim Furyk
2003 US Open*

Players

Tommy Aaron
Jim Ahern
Billy Andrade
Tommy Armour III
Andy Bean
Frank Beard
Chip Beck
Notah Begay
Deane Beman
Jim Benepe
Homero Blancas
Julius Boros
Michael Bradley
Mark Brooks
Billy Ray Brown
George Burns
Bob Byman
Curt Byrum
Joe Campbell
Jim Carter
Ron Cerrudo
Brandel Chamblee
Bobby Clampett
Keith Clearwater
John Cook
Fred Couples
Ben Crane
Ben Crenshaw
Terry Diehl
Allen Doyle
David Duval
Danny Edwards
David Eger
Steve Elkington
Bob Estes
Brad Faxon
Ed Fiori
Marty Fleckman
Steve Flesch
John Fought
Fred Funk
Jim Furyk
Jim Gallagher
Robert Gamez
Matt Gogel

Jay Haas

Scott Hoch

Hubert Green
Gary Hallberg
Phil Hancock
Mark Hayes
Tim Herron
Scott Hoch
Charles Howell III
David Ishii
Joe Inman
John Inman
Don Iverson
Lee Janzen
Steve Jones
Tom Jones
Gary Koch
Billy Kratzert
Tom Lehman
Justin Leonard
Bruce Lietzke
Davis Love III
Steve Lowrey
Mark Lye
Andy Magee
Jeff Maggert
John Mahaffey
Billy Mayfair
Len Mattiace
Jim McGovern
Rocco Mediate
Phil Mickelson
Allen Miller
Gil Morgan
Mike Morley
John Morse
Jodie Mudd
Bob Murphy
Jack Nicklaus
Mike Nicolette
Andy North
David Ogrin
Arnold Palmer
Chris Perry
Peter Persons
Mark Pfeil

Bruce Lietzke

Dan Pohl
Johnny Pott
Dillard Pruitt
Tom Purtzer
Mike Reid
Phil Rodgers
Bill Rogers
John Rollins
Jack Rule
Tom Sieckman
Jay Sigel
Joey Sindelar
Tony Sills
Jim Simons
Scott Simpson
Jeff Sluman
Craig Stadler
Curtis Strange
Steve Stricker
Hal Sutton
Leonard Thompson
Bob Tway
Howard Twitty
Stan Utley
Scott Verplank
Bobby Wadkins
Lanny Wadkins
Art Wall
Mark Wiebe
Willie Wood
Tiger Woods
Kermit Zarley

Rocco Mediate

Players

U.S. Amateur Champions

Buddy Alexander
Deane Beman
Stanley Bishop
William C. Campbell
Richard D. Chapman
John Cook
Gary Cowan
Bubba Dickerson
Charles Evans, Jr.
John Fought
Vinnie Giles
John Harris
Hank Kuehne
Justin Leonard
Billy Mayfair
Steve Melnyk
Phil Mickelson
Robert J. Murphy
Jack Nicklaus
Arnold Palmer
Fred Ridley
Hillman Robbins, Jr.
Jay Sigel
Craig Stadler
Hal Sutton
Scott Verplank
Lanny Wadkins
Tiger Woods

Hank Kuehne won the 2000 U.S. Amateur

In 1916 Chick Evans won the U.S. Open and U.S. Amateur titles. He won the US Amateur again in 1920.

NCAA Champions

Billy Ray Brown
Clark Burroughs
Joe Campbell
Alejandro Canizares
Jim Carter
Bob Clark
Ron Commans
Dick Crawford
Ben Crenshaw
Todd Demsey
Marty Fleckman
Jay Haas
Gary Hallberg
Charles Howell III
John Inman
Justin Leonard
John Mahaffey
Troy Matteson
Phil Mickelson
Bob Murphy
Jack Nicklaus
Hillman Robbins
Phil Rodgers
Scott Simpson
Terry Small
Curtis Strange
Scott Verplank
Charles Warren
Brian Watts
Tiger Woods
Kermit Zarley

British Amateur Champions

Dean Beman
Richard D. Chapman
Vinnie Giles
Steve Melnyk
Dick Siderowf
Jay Sigel

Steve Melnyk won the U.S. Amateur and the British Amateur

Alejandro Canizares 2004 NCAA Champion

Players

U.S. Mid Amateur Champions

Jerry Courville
David Eger
Danny Green
Jim Holtgrieve
Tim Jackson
Bill Loeffler
Michael Podolak
Jay Sigel
Nathan Smith
Jeff Thomas
Danny Yates

Nathan Smith
2003 U.S. Mid-Amateur Champion

Tim Jackson
1994 U.S. Mid-Amateur Champion

U.S. Junior Champions

Don Bisplinghoff
Mike Brannan
Bob Byman
John Crooks
David Duval
Scott Erickson
Don Hurter
Gary Koch
Jack Larkin
Hunter Mahan
Doug Martin
Jim Masserio
Charles McDowell
Shane McMenamy
Dave Nevatt
James Oh
Eddie Pearce
Brett Quigley
Matthew Rosenfeld
Charles Rymer
Gary Sanders
Tim Straub
Jason Widener
Willie Wood
Tiger Woods

1977 U.S. Junior Champion

U.S. Public Links Champions

Don Essig
Ralph Howe
Kevin Johnson
Bill Mayfair
William McDonald
Jody Mudd
Brandt Snedeker
James Sorenson
D.J. Trahan
Guy Yamamoto

Brandt Snedelker
2003 U.S. Public Links

D. J. Trahan
2000 U.S. Public Links Champion

Sunnehanna Members

Tim Crooks

Participant in the 1992 U.S. Junior

William Crooks

Participant in 1962, 1963 1969 U.S. Amateur

Participant in the 1959 National Jaycees Junior

Donald Hall
Participant
1992 U.S. Senior

1990 West Penn Senior Champion

2002 President, Pennsylvania State Golf Association

Jeffrey Hall

1972 West Penn Junior Champion

Participant 1971 and 1972 U.S. Junior

Al Hromulak

1993 West Penn Junior Champion

Madeline Lovette

2003 Pennsylvania Interscholastic Athletic Association (PIAA) Champion

2001 and 2002 U.S. Junior Girls

Emily Marron

Participant in the 1997 and 1998 U.S. Womans Amateur

Women's Head Golf Coach University of North Carolina Greensboro

Caroline O'Connor

Women's Head Golf Coach Stanford University

Sunnehanna Members

Warren Reitz
Participant, 1983 U.S. Junior reached round of sixteen

Participant 1984 U.S. Amateur

George Wolfe
Participant 1977 U.S. Junior

Katrin Wolfe
Participant 2003 U.S. Women's Amateur

J. Philips Saylor

1998 Pennsylvania State Golf Association Senior Champion

1998 West Penn Senior Champion

Todd Thiele
1980 Pennsylvania State Junior Champion

David Yerger
Participant
1983 U.S. Amateur

John Yerger
1977 U.S. Junior, Quarter-finalist

1977 West Penn Junior Champion